# PRAISE
# COMMAND THE CRISIS

Nobody knows about managing crisis better than those of us in the military. Our mettle was tested every day. Angela Billings learned her PR skills under fire in the Air Force—and was even in the Pentagon on 9/11. If you want to know how to manage crisis communication in your company or organization, how to prepare your CEO or exec to handle a press conference, or how to manage the media and the message, look to Angela for insightful lessons on how to remain calm and cool in the face of catastrophe (you never know what challenges you are about to face).

**MIKE MANAZIR,**
Rear Admiral (ret.),
Top Gun, author of *Learn How to Lead to Win*

Whether times are steady or choppy at best, we are wise to follow the lead of Angela Billings. Having witnessed firsthand her calm, rational and organized approach to public relations, I can say with confidence the counsel she provides for managing a crisis will provide safe harbor in the storm. Angela's proven leadership and battle-tested experience give her a strong voice to guide both individuals and organizations through challenging times.

**DAN SMALDONE,**
KY Farm Bureau
Director of Communications

Angela's instrumental leadership strengthened collaboration and partnerships with national media, think tanks, and countless local communities as we navigated telling the national security story in those months and years post 9-11. Her superior skill in media relations and communication strategies was foundational to the integrity of our work, and to my personal achievement. Communication is leadership business, and Angela is the exemplar of this.

**CHRISTY NOLTA,**
former Deputy Assistant Secretary of the
Air Force & former Deputy Director
of the headquarters Air Force staff

Having stood side by side with Angela Billings in 2006 in Kabul, Afghanistan, I can attest to her unparalleled expertise and dedication. Angela's leadership was instrumental to our team winning the public information war. Her book, drawing from her rich experience, is a masterclass in crisis communication and PR strategy. Every page resonates with the discipline and precision I witnessed firsthand during our time in combat. A must-read for anyone serious about understanding the intricacies of effective communication.

Lieutenant Colonel **BRENDAN MAXWELL** (ret.)
Australian Army &
Founder, The Decisive Point

Keeping ahead of the narrative is perhaps the most important skill any leader can have in today's hyperpaced world of crisis communication. Most companies hope only to survive in that world, Angela Billings provides the tools necessary to thrive. Her expertise is unparalleled in managing crisis communication. She has worked in this space at the highest levels of defense and government. From developing a communications strategy and all its supporting elements to how to respond to the unexpected, Angela provides any organization the guidelines necessary to meet communications challenges and always win the battle of the narrative.

Brigadier General **ROB GIVENS** (ret.)
USAF, Thunderbird pilot &
Chief of State for Senator Rand Paul

Angela was always clearheaded and calm in Afghanistan, even as the leader we advised— the wartime 4-star commander—just yards away from our office, met with world leaders and made life-or-death judgments about the Taliban and Al Qaeda.

His decisions to both launch strikes and provide humanitarian aid were complemented by Angela's public information efforts, 24 hours a day. Later in New York City, as the ranking Air Force officer in the nation's largest media market, Angela represented 330,000 Airmen to national media during a major war, and also placed the most senior military leaders on live TV and radio, so Americans knew what their sons and daughters were fighting and dying for.

In every instance, on the quiet days in between crises, Angela was always preparing to get ahead of the next one, by deftly building relationships behind the scenes.

**COLONEL JOHN J. THOMAS (RET.),**
Deputy Director of Public Affairs and
Strategic Communication, National Guard
Bureau & former Director of Public Affairs for
US Central Command

# COMMAND THE CRISIS

## NAVIGATE CHAOS WITH BATTLE-TESTED PUBLIC RELATIONS AND COMMUNICATION STRATEGIES

ANGELA BILLINGS, MBA, APR

Founder, The Virago Circle

ISBN paperback: 979-8-9893847-0-9
ISBN ebook: 979-8-9893847-1-6
ISBN audiobook: 979-8-9893847-2-3
ISBN hard cover 979-8-9893847-3-0

Published by The Virago Circle.
Contact the author at angela@TheViragoCircle.com

# CONTENTS

# ENTER THE WORLD OF CRISIS MANAGEMENT

I arrived at the Air Force press desk, after my walk from our home in Arlington to the Pentagon. It was a clear day, hardly a cloud in the sky. As I made my way up the well-worn steps, I thought of the day ahead of me. I had my first interview set up with a general officer about space operations that afternoon.

My infatuation with the Pentagon, the five-sided building situated just across the Potomac River from Washington, DC, and the seat of our nation's government, began early in my career. As a young officer, I traveled to the Pentagon and saw firsthand how communication on a national level worked. I was enamored, to say the least. When the opportunity presented itself to take a job there just after I pinned on major, I jumped at the chance. Not only was I on the Air Force press desk, but I was the primary public affairs adviser to the undersecretary of the Air Force. This was 2001.

We had our morning spin-up at 8:10 a.m. as we did every day. Each officer reported out to the rest of the team what interviews were scheduled, issues we were working on, and any articles in the morning news that might drive our day. The meeting concluded, and we each went about our day coordinating questions and answers, interviews, and the like a busy military press office would handle.

At 8:46 a.m., a plane hit one of the Twin Towers in the World Trade Center complex in New York City. Knowing what I did about airplanes, flight paths, and airspace management, I thought, "How do you fly a plane into a building in the middle of Manhattan?" The New York airports were some of the busiest in the world, and the sheer number of planes traveling the New York skies initially made it seem possible. Maybe the pilot had had a seizure and veered off the flight path.

It wasn't clear initially even what type of plane it was, but as press reporting began to roll in and the footage streamed across the airwaves, there was speculation it was deliberate. When the second plane hit the South Tower at 9:03 a.m., there was no doubt it was a terrorist attack.

The press desk is one long office with half walls running the length of it. You could stand at one end and see all the way to the other, with the top half of those who occupied the cubicles bobbing up and down. My space was on the far-left side, about three-quarters of the way down and closest to the inner ring of the Pentagon on the third floor. Toward the front, multiple televisions were always tuned to the major networks, and today it was wall-to-wall reporting on the World Trade Center crashes. I had stopped to watch and listen in horror and disbelief as much of the world was doing.

The president of the United States, George W. Bush, was notified of the unfolding disaster while visiting an elementary school in Sarasota, Florida, and immediately flown to the nuclear command center at

Offutt Air Force Base in Nebraska. From my days at the 3rd Wing in Alaska, I knew the stress of many presidential visits and the demands of the traveling press corps accompanying him. This stop would no doubt be amplified because of what was clearly an attack. Tensions remained high. There were so many unknowns.

While watching what was unfolding in New York, I had a conversation with a good friend and public affairs officer, Mike. We had worked together earlier in our careers when he needed to promote equipment tested in New Mexico and I was able to handle the job.

Mike looked directly at me and somberly said, "You know, some people say we could be a target here."

I considered what Mike said for a moment and then headed down the length of the room to my desk as my phone rang. I received a call from the reporter who'd scheduled the interview with my space general who asked if, considering what was taking place in New York, our interview was still on. I confidently told him I would check with the general's office and call him right back. No sooner had I laid the phone in the cradle than the third hijacked plane slammed into the Pentagon. It was 9:37 a.m.

My crisis management skills were about to be tested.

# 1

# KINDRED SPIRITS

**M**aybe you're in your first public relations position in a startup company. Or are a veteran PR manager in a Fortune 500 corporation. Possibly a student studying PR. I understand you. I've been precisely where you are today, challenged to be an effective communicator and a valuable member of the management team you're on.

Many roles fall under the public relations or communication purview, each with its own nuance. No matter the title, these roles likely include some strategic communication that focuses on building relationships between your organization and your public, consumer, or client.

Whether your title is corporate communication, integrated marketing, content management, social media management, or crisis or risk management, that role takes on a form unique to the industry you work in and the leadership you work for. The foundation is the same, though, and flexibility in today's changing world is key to success. As a professional communicator, you can and should be knee-deep in the business of building those relationships. You straddle the fence inside your organization and with the public you serve.

You've got a grasp of the tactics needed for effectively communicating, and you may already have a crisis or two under your belt. You may also be frustrated with a leadership team that doesn't seem in tune with what is unfolding on social media or have an appreciation for the press calls you're fielding. Each member of the leadership team holds a piece of the puzzle in a crisis, and you need everybody on the same page behind the proposed strategy. How do you get them there? Step into your role, no matter the title, and earn the trust of your CEO and other members of your leadership team.

You may already be overwhelmed managing speaking engagements, fielding media calls, reviewing copy to update your web page, and answering myriad questions on your social media platforms. Your team is talented but they are strapped, too, and one of them called in sick today. Your president or CEO has three public events this afternoon and you've got to cover them all. You're on your way to lunch when you receive a phone call from your favorite reporter about a fuel spill. Your product is recalled because of safety concerns. Or a member of your leadership team is accused of mishandling finances inside your organization.

Your list of to-dos just went out the window and you must address what is in front of you and your company right now. Your brand's reputation is at risk. You have to develop a plan and actively manage the crisis or the organization and your CEO simply won't survive.

If you've never been tested under fire—bad press, a corporate scandal, a pandemic, consumer recall, faulty equipment, a misdirected tweet, airplane crash, missteps, stumbles, and outright gaffes—you will be. That's why you're reading this book.

Welcome to the world of public relations crisis management.

# TAKE STOCK

When something blows up—maybe literally—here are some of the immediate questions to ask yourself and your team when presented with a crisis:

- What is the business doing to correct the problem?
- What is the right way to respond?
- What should we consider before making any statement?
- Whom do we need to talk to?
- What is our next step?
- How do we manage the relationships and egos in our organization to protect our company and secure our role in protecting its brand?

The role of the communicator or public relations manager is not simply to communicate on behalf of the organization you work for. To be a respected member of the leadership team, you have to be familiar with each division and every process your company uses. You may not know every minor detail, but a working knowledge of your mission, products, services, and processes will better equip you as the primary communicator for your organization. Your working knowledge of your organization is where you create real value to your boss.

Over my Air Force career, I had to pivot many times as my jobs changed with the Air Force base where I was stationed and the duties I was assigned. For starters, I was commissioned a second lieutenant in the Air Force, and my first professional assignment was at Eaker Air Force Base in Blytheville, Arkansas. I was the deputy public affairs officer for a seven-person team. We had B-52 bombers and KC-135 tankers there.

I deployed to Royal Air Force Fairford in the United Kingdom also as the deputy chief of public affairs, though I was in charge for the first two weeks. When I was in recruiting service at Portsmouth, New Hampshire, I oversaw advertising and promotion for recruiting service across New England. When I was the editor of *TIG Brief Magazine* at Kirtland AFB, New Mexico, I edited a magazine for the Air Force Inspection Agency.

The most difficult job I've had was as the chief of public affairs at Elmendorf AFB, near Anchorage, Alaska. I had a ten-member team to support the five flying units housed there. We had three fighter squadrons, an AWACS squadron, and C-130 cargo planes. I was only a captain at the time and the position was designed for a lieutenant colonel, two grades above me. We had a lot of annual exercises across the Pacific Rim like Foal Eagle and real-world deployments like Operation Desert Fox. There were a lot of moving parts and people and I had to stay on my toes.

At the Air Force press desk in the Pentagon, I handled space issues for the undersecretary of the Air Force. I was selected for Air Command Staff College and lived at Maxwell AFB near Montgomery, Alabama, for a year and earned my second master's degree.

While I was in Germany, I worked at United States Air Forces in Europe (USAFE) as the chief of current operations. In Korea, I was the number-two person in charge of all United States and Korean public affairs activities for the 28,000-plus troops stationed there. And in New York, I was the direct liaison with all national media agencies and civic organizations for the Air Force.

After transitioning out of the military in 2012, I worked with several nonprofits before starting my own business, The Virago Circle. I am currently the director of communication for the Kentucky Senate Majority.

Because of this incredible diversity of experience and my passion to pass on my wisdom to those who follow, I have captured some of the learning in this book.

Often, as you may already know or discover, businesses are so focused on building their business that they fail to pause and take stock of what they would do if and when something goes wrong. Whether it's a sense that nothing bad will happen, or an attitude of "we'll deal with the crisis if and when it does," many companies are ill prepared to effectively handle a crisis of any magnitude, which can make or break their company.

The cost of a crisis to you professionally and to your company organizationally is not only measured in lost sales or eroding community good will, but in very real dollars impacting the bottom line. If businesses aren't prepared for a crisis before it happens, this leaves an impression with their customers that the company doesn't care.

Ultimately, it's the CEO or president who is responsible in a crisis. It's also the responsibility of the public relations or communication professionals to carve out time and put thought into the most likely and worst possible scenarios you may have to handle. If you want to keep your current job, fleeing is not really an option. How you handle these stressors largely determines your success or failure.

You're familiar with the term *fight-or-flight instincts*. When faced with a perceived threat, our instincts to either stay and fight or flee a stressful situation involve the part of our brain called the amygdala, one of two almond-shaped clusters whose primary role is to process memory, decision-making, and emotional responses; these responses typically include fear, anxiety, and even aggression.

You've likely experienced all these emotions. You may also have experienced any one of these scenarios:

- Your boss comes into your office first thing and says she needs this proposal updated with new product information by the end of the day.

- You have to decipher the company financials and develop talking points for the next board meeting.
- Research is needed for a speaking engagement your CEO has tomorrow; you've got to develop slides to depict why your company is far superior to your closest competitor.
- The product rollout timeline has been accelerated. You have to develop the web content and post it within the next twenty-four hours.
- Forget the news release you just finalized; your company was acquired by another company and now your job is at risk.

All of these demands could elicit an instinctual flight response.

## CASE STUDY: SOUTHWEST AIRLINES

**The Setup**

This was a classic case of a perfect storm. Winter Storm Elliott moved across the United States in December 2022 and forced record flight cancelations across the nation. Most airlines recovered quickly, within a day or so, but passengers on Southwest Airlines were stranded in airports for days as the holiday quickly approached. Southwest canceled 60 percent of its flights, approximately 16,000 flights in an eleven-day period.

## The Response

Bad weather aside, it became apparent this significant failure was primarily because of an antiquated computer system that couldn't match available crews with existing flights.

## The Result

Negative. Southwest's antiquated computer system failed to match passengers with available flights. Limping along with this outdated system from the 1990s demonstrated poor foresight by management on the digital infrastructure needed to manage such a dynamic industry that had grown exponentially over the last three decades.

The Department of Transportation (DOT) launched its investigation in January 2023 into Southwest for "unrealistic flight scheduling," which is prohibited by the Federal Aviation Administration (FAA). Under DOT rules, canceled flights must be promptly rebooked or fully refunded.

The question was if Southwest's actions could be considered an unfair and deceptive practice under federal law. Did they know they would be unable to fulfill their cascading bookings with their current staffing situation? The Department of Justice (DOJ) jumped on the investigation bandwagon in April to determine if there was any criminal activity associated with the airline's December meltdown.

**The Response**

- Southwest CEO Bob Jordan was quick to apologize and promised to make everything right with all customers impacted by their inability to get passengers to their intended destinations.
- He and others inside Southwest's leadership leveraged recorded videos to their team members and customers, which they posted on their web page.
- Southwest also included action plans on its web page to indicate the improved processes they were implementing.
- In one video, COO Andrew Watterson admitted flawed policies. He emphasized all expenses customers had related to their cancelations would be reimbursed.
- Jordan promised to upgrade its winter infrastructure to be more responsive to changing weather patterns and implement software updates to handle demands.

**My Take**

I couldn't find footage of a single live press conference, which I see as a significant missed opportunity. This approach could have been a deliberate attempt to control the message and protect their leadership. If that was the case, it worked. Southwest Airlines's initial lack of transparency bruised their standing with the competition. The DOT and DOJ investigations drew into question their corporate culture, honesty, and integrity.

Jordan stated Southwest was keeping DOT informed, as well as their board of directors. Media reports indicated more direct communication with its team members and customers would have helped mitigate the crisis and keep their brand intact.

In comparison with other airlines, Southwest failed their customers and left them stranded with time spent in the airport instead of with their families. Southwest should benchmark against other airlines that recovered far more quickly. Clearly, they need to hire additional IT experts and build a more responsive infrastructure, train their employees, and communicate with them to ensure a crisis like this doesn't happen again.

Since Southwest boasted a $6.103 billion gross profit in 2022, a 13.29 percent increase from 2021, they can well afford whatever the costs are to get their infrastructure up to industry standards.

I found far more statements from the DOT, and none from the DOJ confirming their participation in the investigation. Again, this may be deliberate, but Southwest is allowing others to control their narrative and fill their public-facing void. Southwest should hold regularly scheduled press updates to enhance transparency and inform the public regularly on process improvements. Communicating to their board and stockholders may have been taking place behind the scenes. Upgrades taking place internally would require training employees across all business lines. Southwest will also need a robust internal communication strategy to match what the company is saying publicly.

# THE IMPORTANCE OF PLANNING

According to a *Forbes* article "YEC Council Post: Pre-emptively Planning for a PR Crisis: How to Protect Your Company" by Evan Nierman, businesses without a PR crisis plan may find themselves playing defense and fending off criticism instead of controlling the narrative and setting a path for crisis recovery.

Planning for the worst and preparing to face the most likely obstacles will help you control communications and protect your company's most prized possession: its reputation.

First, you must overcome your primal instinct to run in the opposite direction. Fortunately, there is also an accompanying sensation, a response Daniel Goleman coined in *Emotional Intelligence* in 1995, called the amygdala hijack—our brain's radar for threat. Goleman describes the almost instantaneous response taking milliseconds to occur as being manageable. Your inherent instinct to keep predators at bay in prehistoric times can be managed and controlled. Planning for your next crisis today sets you up for success when bad things occur and will allow you to think through how the company will respond.

We train how we will fight in the military every day. Consider this book your initial training. You, too, can prepare now for how you will respond to the crisis. Part of what makes an effective crisis manager is the ability to move past any possible hijack and remain calm, despite the emotions you may naturally feel.

How you move past a hijack is quite simple—by planning for your next crisis *today.*

# HOW TO PREPARE TODAY

Every crisis presents an opportunity for success, an equal opportunity for failure, and in a very public way. What you say or the information you release publicly is for quote and will be forever captured on the internet. Here's the good news, though: what doesn't kill you makes you stronger. A crisis is also an opportunity to bring value to your organization. There are steps you can take *today* to better prepare for and even improve your company's chances of weathering the next crisis. Take a moment to think about the following:

- What will you do when your organization experiences a serious incident?
- Who is on your crisis communication team, your quick reaction force, and who will actively manage the crisis?
- Who will you inform immediately?
- How will you respond publicly?
- How are you going to handle the barrage of tweets or Facebook posts you're sure to receive?
- What about the persistent public outcry because your company is not taking action?

- How will you manage the flow of information internally and what will you say publicly?
- How will you help your president or CEO navigate through this crisis so your brand remains intact?

If you are the communication expert, the public relations manager, or even the marketing representative in your organization, the CEO should look to you for help managing the crisis. As a professional communicator, you can and should be intimately involved in whatever the response is.

During my military career, I have performed under extreme pressure in seemingly unrealistic time constraints almost daily. I hope my combat-proven experiences can help you, whether you are in a corporate, small business, nonprofit, or educational business setting.

Looking ahead, in the following chapters I discuss the importance of communicating with your internal team and assigning roles when managing a crisis. We will look at the role of social media and how tweets and posts have changed the very nature of handling real-time crises.

You'll want to establish relationships with reporters, and I'll tell you how. We will walk through crisis communication, how to recover and salvage your brand, and end up with a discussion of your professional advancement. I'll circle back to 9/11 at the Pentagon and that horrible day.

We in the military love checklists, so I've included a few handy ones in this book prompting you to take actions *today* to make you a more effective crisis communicator.

We are the sum of our experiences; mine include battle-tested crisis management during combat. Yours may revolve around product malfunctions or poor management decisions. Whatever it is, I'm in the next crisis with you!

## CASE STUDY: BREONNA TAYLOR KILLING

### The Setup

On March 13, 2020, the same day the world essentially shut down because of a global pandemic, a tragedy took place in Louisville, Kentucky. Breonna Taylor, a young Black woman, was killed when Louisville Metropolitan Police entered her apartment on a drug tip. Kenneth Walker, her boyfriend, was at Taylor's apartment and fired upon police before officers breached the front door.

Taylor was killed and the questionable manner in which the search warrant was obtained and the raid executed incited riots in Louisville and other cities across the nation. There was no body camera footage from the raid to answer the immediate questions of who did what and when. Increasing city crime created a strained relationship between LMPD, its Chief of Police Steve Conrad, and Louisville Mayor Greg Fischer.

## The Response

- Officers involved in the raid were put on administrative leave but not charged until September 2020. Fischer fired Conrad in June 2022 and in September was delivered a no-confidence vote himself by the Louisville Metro Council.
- The Kentucky Air National Guard (KYANG) was called up to help manage protests and riots. During those riots, another Black citizen, David McAtee, was shot and killed at the hands of LMPD and KYANG in June, again with no body camera footage.
- Policies regarding body camera footage were implemented, but with the McAtee shooting and no existing footage, it was clear standard operating procedures were not enforced.

## The Result

Extremely negative outcome.

Questionable police actions—the manner in which the search warrant was issued and the lack of available and releasable body camera footage—created suspicion and speculation.

This situation was poorly managed from the get-go and indicated internal problems within the police department.

## My Take

Louisville police and the city of Louisville lacked a deliberate process to investigate and had no communication strategy to convey their actions to the public. Their lack of transparency and questionable practices fueled racial tensions not only in Louisville but across the nation. Leadership should have provided regular public updates on their actions through regular press conferences.

Little information and insensitive posturing by leadership fueled suspicions of police brutality against people of color. The strained relationship between the police and the mayor exacerbated tension felt from the pandemic lockdown and ensuing city riots. If the police chief had taken personal accountability and improved their internal practices immediately, tensions may have eased sooner.

The KYANG was both ill-equipped and poorly trained to handle the riots using common crowd control practices. Eventually, the FBI stepped in to investigate.

# 2

# JUMP INTO MY FOXHOLE: BRING YOUR TEAM INTO THE CRISIS WITH YOU

**F**reezing cold wind whipped across my face as I departed the military plane after landing at the mothballed base at Royal Air Force Fairford, England. Fresh out of college and with the United States already well into Desert Storm, I was part of the initial leadership team that flew from Eaker Air Force Base in Blytheville, Arkansas, into England ahead of the B-52 bombers, KC-135 tankers, and the people who would follow.

As the lead communicator for your organization representing your business, your role is far more important than simply communicating for your organization, as I was about to find out. Your role is to reduce your company's risk by developing the solutions to whatever the problem is, managing it, and mitigating the crisis and potential damage to your brand. You have to identify the key people who will be a part of your crisis response team or a quick reaction force—these are leaders across your lines of business—through the crisis.

In the days following our arrival at Fairford, the remaining leadership including the wing commander, legal counsel, personnel management or human resources, pilots, maintenance, and support troops trickled in. Those who were in these top positions became our de facto crisis response team. Six months behind the initial staging that had already occurred during Desert Shield and the current military operations of Desert Storm, which began on January 15, we were already behind schedule and in crisis.

The intensity was high, the sense of urgency great, as US troops in Iraq were at risk. We could feel the sense of urgency like the blast of heat you feel when you open the hot oven door. It hits you in the face and gets your immediate attention.

Leadership prepared for hundreds of troops and equipment to arrive from many locations, establish aircraft maintenance and flying operations, and meet the local civic leaders who would be critical to mission success.

I was already in my own personal crisis mode, and I imagine you have also been hit with a crisis already in full swing. Outside of the physical building, there was no public affairs office, no computers, supplies, pens, or paper, and aside from me, no people to communicate with about our mission. We anticipated what our forces would need to contribute to a successful campaign against Saddam Hussein. And I needed to communicate effectively to our troops, manage media operations, and establish relationships with local leadership.

## INTERNAL AUDIENCE

I, along with my operations commander, assessed our immediate needs. First among them was communicating effectively inside our own organization to our internal audience. The base newsletter was important then because airplane maintenance chiefs and supply technicians spent little time, if any, in email. Forget embracing technology. I had to find a way to print hard copies of a newsletter with the most basic information in it about when the dining hall would be serving meals and when a troop could expect the shuttle to get them back and forth from their bunk to their workplace.

Company intranets, which are workplace communication professionals' second choice for effective internal communication methods, may prove more effective, provided employees can—and do—access them. Dynamic Signal's research found communication professionals surveyed cited company intranet as the second most effective form of internal communication, behind email and ahead of social media, breakroom posters, and mobile apps.

With communication challenges posed by COVID-19, Zoom, WebEx, and Microsoft Teams became the platforms of choice for receiving company information directly. They also became the tether to staying connected professionally and personally when we couldn't interact in person.

Even though email remains the primary way most people receive company information, technology development has provided a plethora of apps to communicate quickly with your entire workforce. Deskless employees continue to rise and there's no reason to believe that trend will change.

Since transitioning out of the military, I've worked with clients who've leveraged different apps as a quick way to update team members during crises. When I worked with a major university, we used the Google Suite and Google Meet. When I was with a nonprofit and a political leadership team, their preferred crisis app was GroupMe. Slack is another app providing collaboration and instant communication with your team.

Think about what your communication needs are, what complements how your team communicates, and make sure everyone is connected. Have your team members download the apps, turn notifications on, and get comfortable with their capability, so when you need it, you have established instant communication.

Perhaps you have a company dashboard or a daily internal bulletin you can leverage during a crisis. When I was in Korea, we held a daily operational meeting in person with all key staff to share information and collaborate across all lines of business. As the chief communication officer, you absolutely should be a part of this daily touchpoint so when a crisis occurs, you're in immediate contact with key leadership and have a platform with which to share information quickly.

To illustrate the importance of effectively communicating with your internal audience, I'll share an oversight I made in coordinating with my own. After transitioning out of the military, my first role was with a major researcher who was going to publish an academic paper with extraordinary developments for people with spinal cord injuries. I did all the coordination with the university associated with the research, the rehabilitation center affiliated with it, a significant research foundation, and another local research partner.

We coordinated the date of release and planned to promote the research in New York so we could leverage the major television network stations there. The research made a huge media splash, and I was receiving calls from all the major networks, wire services, and academic magazines. The mistake I made, though, was not telling my counterpart with our local research partner the specific date of the release. She didn't even know we'd gone to New York and didn't have the latest guidance and talking points.

While there was only one person I left out of the conversation, it was a key person on our internal team who could have helped me manage the demand for information about this significant research. It was a valuable lesson learned.

# WORKING WITH PEERS

Perhaps you have needed to coordinate with peers internally to develop an approach or gather information. For military public affairs, it's a balancing act to protect classified information or perhaps for you safeguarding company proprietary information, while still remaining transparent to the public. In my case, I developed public affairs guidance on space control, a philosophical approach to managing our space assets, to dismantle conspiracy theories of supposed world domination of all satellites.

Shortly after I arrived at the Pentagon, an executive and I talked about the need for space control public affairs guidance. I carved out time to develop the right words to convey managing space assets to share publicly without compromising our high-tech classified capabilities. For about six weeks, I met with peers and subject-matter experts and developed a good first draft of the top messages, likely questions and answers, and parameters for the public affairs guidance for the Department of Defense.

I coordinated our response with key leadership at the Pentagon—those who would be using our message in media interviews and congressional testimony. Before we talked about it publicly with the Pentagon press, we distributed the guidance to the field to ensure every service at all military bases understood the guidance and talking points to stress. We established our release date for the new guidance. Informing my peers well ahead of the release date was key to consistent messages at all levels of the military branches and the Department of Defense.

It's also important to ensure your team, though they are all experts in their field, understand they are not official spokespeople for the business. When managing a crisis, you typically want to control the narrative by having one person serve as the face and voice for the organization. This is often your president or CEO who demonstrates accountability and responsibility during a crisis.

Make sure your internal team understands the importance of speaking with one voice as you manage your way through a crisis. I'll provide more details about planning a crisis press conference and setting up media interviews in chapter 6.

The lines between internal communication and social media have blurred significantly during the past decade or more. In the next chapter, I'll discuss how social media has changed how we communicate during a crisis, especially as it shortened response time and made effectively communicating during a crisis even more critical.

## WHERE THINGS WENT WRONG

**Bottom Line Up Front: Recognize there are some things you simply can't control.**

It was our first media event after the initial launch of B-52s over downtown Baghdad. The international press was there to cover their return and our contribution to the fall of Saddam Hussein. The wing commander was on the mission. He wanted to engage with reporters. We'd credentialed the media to make sure they represented legitimate media outlets and invited them to interview the wing commander.

Most everything went well until the end when a television reporter asked about the "indiscriminate bombing of the B-52."

My commander was taken off guard, almost aghast the reporter would pose this question. His response was, "I don't know what you mean about indiscriminate. Our analysis showed precision when we dropped our bombs. They hit their intended targets."

The interview ended shortly thereafter. As we were packing things up, my commander pulled me to the side and said, "Well, where did her question about indiscriminate bombing come from?"

I asked, "What do you mean?"

He said, "Why would she ask me about indiscriminate bombing when our bombs are very precise. We have all this technology available. We have our mission plan. We have intelligence to make sure we hit our intended targets."

My simple response was, "She's a reporter, and asking probing questions. That's her job."

It was almost as if he thought I should know everything a reporter would ask ahead of time. My commander handled it well and refuted the assertion the reporter was making. Don't automatically accept what the reporter provides as the gospel truth.

I learned two valuable lessons that day. One, even though you try, you can't anticipate everything a reporter will ask. Two, be prepared to defend yourself and your brand when a reporter says something you know to be false.

# WHAT YOU NEED TO KNOW

- Before a crisis occurs, establish your crisis response team. This will be your CEO, COO, legal counsel, human resources, and, of course, communication or PR. Depending on what your crisis is, it may also include other subject-matter experts.
- Your internal audience, those inside your organization, are always one of your key audiences during a crisis. You can reach your internal audience quickly and readily by way of a simple email, company intranet, or one of the many available apps. Make sure everyone is connected in at least one way.
- Leverage internal communication platforms. Use the company's digital channel, intranet, company newsletter, or other platforms unique to your organization. If you don't have an internal platform for your workforce, consider developing one today to be well established before the next crisis occurs.
- Use any of the myriad available apps to communicate instantly. Assume everything you tell your internal public will also eventually make its way onto social media—and the press—so keep your messaging consistent across all channels.
- Internal audiences are not official spokespeople for your company. While they need to

remain informed to perpetuate information flowing out of the crisis, they should not be talking to the press unless you set them up for an interview.

- Set realistic expectations for your leadership. While you can prepare for a media engagement, you can't control what comes out of a reporter's mouth.

# 3

# I READ IT ON SOCIAL MEDIA: LEVERAGE THE PLATFORMS YOU SOMETIMES HATE

While working with the Kentucky Senate Majority, I had to manage ample crises involving drag queens and book bans, bathrooms and gender pronouns. Let me explain.

Kentucky is a part-time legislature. From January through April, legislators travel from their districts on Monday and spend the rest of the week in Frankfort, drafting legislation, listening to testimony, and passing bills. The supermajority builds veto days into the calendar to protect priority legislation from the governor's veto so they have time to legally override priority bills.

During the 2023 legislative session, the climate was intense with numerous culture war legislation issues dubbed anti-LGBTQ+ by the liberal minded and parental rights by the conservatives. Topics included drag queen shows and possible book banning, bathroom use and preferred gender pronouns, and which soccer team middle schoolers could play on. If you watched any cable news, you saw this unfold.

Protests were staged before committee meetings, and the halls between committee rooms were flooded with opposing interest groups. Everyone on my team was operating at a feverish pace for an extended period of time, and the tone was contentious at best.

Parents were upset the public school system encouraged students to hide their gender preference or sexual orientation in secrecy. Children were allowed to use the bathroom or locker room they associated with their gender, causing turmoil especially for young girls. Teachers were pitted against parents. The administration and education commissioner suggested if teachers would not refer to students by their preferred pronouns, they should seek other employment.

Protests against this legislation, Senate Bill 150, and another bill, Senate Bill 5, aptly referred to as Harmful to Minors, came to a head in the final days of the session. SB 5 laid out the process by which any parent could appeal to the school system to limit material they deemed inappropriate for their children to be exposed to. Material depicting sexual acts and addressing sexual orientation in elementary and middle school was the focus.

As both bills made their way through the process, tensions increased inside and outside the legislative chambers. Protests on the Capitol steps took place. The galleries were full of interest groups opposing and supporting the bills. Arrests were made for those interrupting floor proceedings.

Then another story broke.

The Twitter account of a senator from western Kentucky was hacked. Explicit posts were made. The hacker began trolling pornographic sites, following and liking sexually explicit profiles. A reporter called me with the story. How could the same senator carrying legislation to limit sexually explicit materials to minors engage in such questionable activity from his own Twitter handle?

I spoke with the senator. This story had surfaced eighteen months prior and had been addressed then. At that time, the senator told the reporter he had been hacked, had notified Twitter, hired an IT expert to scour and scrub his activity, changed his password, and thought his account had been restored. The story fizzled out.

Nothing had appeared in print earlier, but this reporter was now with a different agency and had a different editor who saw merit to the story. The general counsel and I sat down with the reporter and editor to discover what they thought they had. They provided screenshots of past Twitter activity. The situation was not good.

Preparing for the worst, I circled back with the senator. I immediately conducted media training as he had not had any experience with a contentious attack like this. He got more comfortable defending his actions and his remedy to the hack. Despite my best effort, I was unable to persuade the press to skip the story. I provided a statement explaining what had transpired and discouraged the senator from speaking with them again. The story ran the next day.

I touched base with the senator once more. He had received several requests for interviews from his local television stations. We reviewed our strategy and his defense and set up three separate Zoom interviews later that day.

Over the roar of the protests in the Capitol halls, the senator stepped off the floor to a side office and explained what had happened with the hack. It was a two-day news story. We addressed the situation head on and managed the narrative. The senator handled himself well and explained what had transpired.

Despite intense pressure, heightened emotions, and stressful testimony, on one hand, I had to step away from the fray, conduct on-the-spot media training, and guide my senator through this crisis.

# HIGH TENSION ON THE DMZ

I was prepared for such high tension in the Kentucky legislature because of earlier crises in international situations like this one.

I'd been in South Korea for about three weeks. I was still getting used to the operations tempo and figuring out whom to coordinate with when startling news came across the wire. A South Korean woman vacationing at the five-star hotel in North Korea wandered too far down the beach and was shot and killed by a North Korean soldier. Really? South Koreans actually vacationed in communist North Korea?

There is no peace treaty, and the two countries are separated by a heavily guarded demilitarized zone, the DMZ. I could think of other countries in Southeast Asia, like Thailand or Japan, as possible vacation destinations where you aren't under constant armed guard. I physically shuddered as I considered the location I had volunteered for.

I began to question my new assignment. The job at Yongsan in Seoul, South Korea, was challenging and arguably dangerous, and I had brought my family with me. Since Korea was technically a high-risk overseas location, being assigned there meant I would not deploy to another active combat zone while there. Having returned from my Afghanistan deployment the previous year, this seemed like an attractive option, but now I wasn't so sure.

Perhaps you have taken on a perfectly fitting role initially, but shortly after joining the team, you begin having second thoughts. You could simply quit your job if it wasn't what you'd hoped for, but the financial ramifications and potential bruise on your personal brand may be too great. In the military, quitting a job after moving with your family wasn't really an option. No matter the circumstance, we must face crisis head on, keep our wits about ourselves, and manage it.

The Korean peninsula is a unique place. Split in two after the Korean War ended with an armistice agreement in 1953, the two countries remain at odds even today. The north is aligned with the world's largest communist country, China. The southern half is surrounded on three sides by seawater and remains a free democracy. When the Korean War ended, families were literally split in two with fathers, sons, and brothers on opposite sides when an armistice was declared, and the DMZ was established.

Tensions are high on the peninsula, and the United States military remains in the south to keep communism at bay. Every action or military exercise South Korea takes is viewed as a threat to North Korea, and skirmishes between the two countries occur often. Most military members assigned to Korea would go alone for a year, leave their families back in the United States, and return to the US after that year. Others in key positions brought their families with them for at least a two-year commitment.

I was fortunate to have my husband and two young daughters with me—at least I thought so before that shooting in North Korea.

# INTRODUCING SOCIAL MEDIA

When the Pew Research Center began tracking social media adoption in 2005, just 5 percent of American adults used at least one social media platform. By 2011, that share rose to half of all Americans, and today 72 percent of the public uses some type of social media.

Facebook and YouTube are the most widely used online platforms today, followed by WhatsApp, Instagram, WeChat, and TikTok. Facebook Messenger and Douyin are holding respectable positions in the market while X (formerly Twitter) and Pinterest are waning in popularity from just a year prior. And Threads is gaining traction. For many users, social media is part of their daily routine. Seven in ten Facebook users, and around six in ten Instagram and Snapchat users visit their sites at least once a day.

I joined Facebook about the same time Pew Research began tracking social media data. I was stationed overseas with two little ones and primarily wanted to share photos with their grandparents in the United States. Our commander was interested in what service members were saying about coming to Korea alone or accompanied with their family members. As our headquarters didn't have a Facebook page yet, we launched one to gauge interest from service members about bringing their families with them and staying in Korea for a regular three-year tour.

The public affairs team empowered a more junior member to set up the profile, provide content, and engage on the platform. We gave direction and guidance, parameters around what he could post and began interacting on the platform, primarily with family members to the military member stationed in Korea.

We held online discussions about the state of families there and those who were unable to bring their families with them. The public affairs team developed talking points and worked with our human resource professionals for live chat during the online discussion. This was a huge hit and eye-opening to leadership. The great benefit of social media platforms is they provide a direct link to the people you want most to receive your information. They also provide immediate, unfiltered feedback and built-in analytics.

While our information about social media usage was anecdotal, public affairs provided key information to our commander based on the comments received through online discussions. It was such a success, we scheduled subsequent online discussions and learned more about the many families who wanted to come to Korea. The commander's appetite was ripe for direct communication with both troops and their family members. Since more people wanted to come to Korea, we would move forward with making certain Korean locations with the needed infrastructure like housing and childcare open to anyone interested in bringing their family with them.

Because of the online discussions and the information on Facebook, we received numerous media questions about the discontented families who could not come to Korea. This sparked a public debate on just how safe South Korea was. As I mentioned, I had my own doubts too. To ensure consistency in our messages, we placed the information on social media, matched the news releases distributed to the press with the same, and hung the information on our web page. This new element demanded time and attention from the team and changed our own operations tempo.

After the online discussions ended, the demand for information did not. Families were frustrated and wanted to know when we would change Korean tours so they could move with the service member. The commander used information gleaned from Facebook and took it to the Pentagon, where military policy is written, and pushed for "tour normalization."

Tour normalization was changing the regular one-year assignment in South Korea to a regular three-year tour. That would mean any service member could bring their families with them just like those stationed in Germany, Japan, and England, or any base in the United States.

There was such interest from family members willing to risk living in Korea while their service members were stationed there, we created a wait list. While initially appealing, this particular decision created another crisis demanding management. There was such a demand with service members remaining on the wait list so long, their time in Korea was over, and the opportunity had passed.

Negative comments rolled in, and while it was tempting to delete them, we resisted. If we deleted comments, we would lose the all-important transparency companies strive for through social media engagement. Active management required more time and attention, so we pulled in another team member to help manage the volume. I provided oversight, checked in regularly with the two team members managing the exchange, and delivered analytics to key leadership.

The comments were seemingly unending and continued to be managed from Korea while our primary audience was back in the United States. We provided the key steps we were taking to make tours in Korea a regular three-year tour. Our HR subject-matter experts remained engaged with updates, and public affairs continued to answer questions with as much information as we could share. We strived to maintain transparency by being responsive to every comment.

It was a challenge to address the same issue or answer questions seventeen or more different ways.

We conveyed empathy to frustrated family members who simply missed their spouses and were worn thin with family separation. Tour normalization continued to drain time and resources from other mission needs, but once we began the engagement on the platform, we soon realized we would never be able to stop. Social media was here to stay.

## SCHEDULE YOUR SOCIAL ENGAGEMENT

We didn't have it in Korea at the time, but now there are so many social media management tools available to help you communicate more effectively in a crisis. You're likely using one or more in your daily operations rhythm already, just as I've depicted in my crisis decision matrix in chapter 6.

I typically plan out social media engagement monthly by identifying key events, crafting messages to amplify regularly, and ensuring consistent engagement. To maintain relevance to your audience and timeliness of your engagement, schedule specific posts a week out. You can do this on Friday afternoon for the following week or first thing Monday morning, depending on your personal rhythm. Be sure you tag organizations you collaborate with or that like to participate in your discussion and research relevant hashtags before you post.

Think about those who care about your business or are impacted by the service you provide. If something bad happens, what will be important for them to know? What is the best way to provide information directly about the crisis at hand? What will you do to mitigate the situation and keep people safe? What are you doing to keep this horrible occurrence from happening again?

Pew Research tells us social media use has increased exponentially; in fact, most users spend more than two hours a day on their preferred platform. Now, users in China, India, and the United States consume the most social media, and Facebook remains the top social media platform for the majority of Americans. YouTube, WhatsApp, Instagram, WeChat, and TikTok are other social media platforms your potential consumers are receiving information from—all platforms you can leverage with built-in algorithms and analytics.

Leverage available platforms but recognize you won't necessarily use every single platform every single time. Our family members in the United States, by and large, were on Facebook as it was one of the earliest platforms. Think through the available platforms today, determine where your target audience resides, and meet them there.

## SOCIAL MEDIA IN CRISIS

Social media has become a standard way to communicate during a crisis. While you must leverage available platforms, a comprehensive crisis communication effort can't stand solely on social media alone. You still have to complement the speed of social media with more traditional communication methods like a thoughtful press release and preparing your key people for a live press conference. I cover both of those elements in chapter 6.

I've worked with various clients since my transition from military service to the private sector. While I initially avoided the platform, I've leveraged Twitter and more extensively TweetDeck to manage tweets, as well as simultaneously posting to Facebook and Instagram for greater efficiency.

Typically, we schedule our posts a week out as a way to manage the dynamic information flow. There was an instance when we planned out posts for regularly scheduled events when a senior member passed away. While he was ill for some time waging his personal battle with cancer, his passing meant we needed to adjust our tweets and other social media posts so as not to interfere with our tribute to him. We went back into the management tools and adjusted the schedule to keep it timely and remain relevant. You can and should do the same.

## WHAT YOU NEED TO KNOW

- Find out where your key audiences are and leverage your ability to communicate directly with them one-on-one. Recognize you won't use every single platform every single time.

- Internal audiences serve as brand ambassadors on social media and reinforce the information you release with their own networks. Encourage them to stay engaged on social media to perpetuate the messages you put out with traditional releases.
- You may be tempted to do so but don't delete negative comments. Use social media listening—the information you glean from social media discussions—to determine if your audience is receiving the information you are releasing. Adjust your communication if needed.
- Assign someone or possibly two team members in a crisis to manage the social media platforms you have a presence on. Train your social media experts. Give them direction and guidance and allow them the flexibility to manage the comments and report back to you with what they learn. Check their responses from time to time as if you are a consumer to be sure they are on track, and course correct if needed.
- Post factual crisis updates frequently, avoiding inflammatory language. Employ your subject-matter experts to ensure information is accurate.
- Think on your feet. During a crisis, leverage social media management and cancel the automatic posts you have planned, update

the schedule, or manually manage your posts until the crisis has subsided.

- Use a content management system (CMS) with an integrated emergency warning system to allow you to send information to all your social media channels in one simple step and from a mobile device.
- Take what you learned through social media and improve your process, operations, or communication standards.

## WHERE THINGS WENT WRONG

**Bottom Line Up Front: As the communication or public relations expert, you are never the story.**

While I was the deputy chief of public affairs at Royal Air Force Fairford in England, the media were wrapping up after interviews held in front of the B-52s and asked me to pose under the wing of one of the planes. Without batting an eye, I obliged. I stood under the wing with my arms suspended above my head as if I, much like Superman, was bearing the entire weight of the plane with my own brute strength.

Cameras were clicking left and right, and I could see flashes going off. After the impromptu photoshoot ended, the major in charge of public affairs abruptly pulled me aside. She left me standing there and turned to ask the media to please not use any of the photos of the junior officer because she was not what the mission was about.

Returning to me as the press were gathering their equipment, she chastised me privately saying I was not the focus of the story and I should never, ever pull a stunt like that again. I haven't.

# 4

# PLAN FOR YOUR
# NEXT CRISIS NOW

**M**y heart was racing and my palms were sweating. My stomach was in knots, and I'd already been to the bathroom twice, after not having slept well the night before.

Today was my first press conference as a spokesperson for NATO's International Security Assistance Force (ISAF). Thirty-two nations had banded together and been at war with the Taliban inside Afghanistan for over six years. I'd been in Kabul at the headquarters for only a few months, and now I was taking the press conference alongside my Afghanistan counterpart.

I checked and double-checked my prepared words. The war effort was in full swing and every day was a new crisis. Everything was a threat to our people and the operation, including the reporters who'd been physically vetted by the bomb dogs at the front gate. The cameras were on and the lights were bright. I felt trepidation as I took to the platform, still hearing the negative thoughts in my head. It was go time and nothing less than perfection was acceptable. I took a seat and a deep breath, a drink of water, and began my opening statement.

Perhaps you've been in a similar PR situation.

# TRAIN LIKE YOU FIGHT

One of the best ways you can add value for your CEO or president is to put them through media training. The media training we conducted at the Pentagon was by far the most in-depth I've participated in, and I've replicated similar training elsewhere since.

I've developed and executed media training throughout my career. Perhaps you've considered doing so yourself or had to on the fly when a crisis occurred. What's important to know is you absolutely should develop media training and rehearse ahead of a crisis. Your training can be a part of a larger tabletop exercise common in businesses that work with government agencies, emergency management, police departments, the airport, or others prone to incidents. It can also be a standalone service you create specific to your business.

There are things you can do today to train your leadership before a crisis hits. Understanding what is important to your boss is critical. Having access to your leadership is also essential. Understanding your business product or service is key to developing the training for others to do the same.

You must have a clear understanding of the mission, and you must have direction and guidance from your CEO or president, to successfully manage a crisis. A lot of great leaders may not appreciate what an effective communication strategy means to their business, so you may have to convince them how important the training is. Realize their vision with the tools, tactics, and strategies that effective crisis communication offers.

You should build a media training program suited to your mission or business operation. And do it before a crisis occurs so you can readily respond when it does. Learn all you can about your business or mission. Does your company have sound operational processes and a structure you can be proud of? If they don't, then perhaps some collective thought by the leadership team should occur before those processes come into question. If your structure is flawed and your people aren't safe in their job, there is little to say publicly to talk your way out of a crisis.

In the Air Force, we have instructions, operational plans, checklists, exercise plans, official forms, technical manuals, slide decks, inspection reports, and after-action reviews. Have the courage to question operational practices to contribute to the improvement of your business overall.

Even with sound business practices, bad things happen. While you may be unable to prevent a crisis from occurring, how you behave ahead of a crisis can largely determine how you emerge from the crisis once it's over. Being transparent and forthcoming with information before a crisis occurs will take some of the wind out of your opponents' sails when a crisis presents itself. There are steps you can take today to better prepare yourself as the spokesperson and your leadership to effectively communicate when something bad happens.

While individual interviews are typically the focus for media preparation, we also developed a full-blown press conference for executives to have the full experience preparing for and delivering answers to tough questions.

With every new presidential administration, there was a slew of new executives appointed to the Pentagon to interface with military leaders, most with little or no experience with the press. While all were technical experts and possessed some level of genius on their own, many were not skilled in communicating before a camera or been exposed to media of any caliber, let alone on a national scale.

Enter Air Force Media Training, the great equalizer. The Air Force training was, by far, the most rigorous, comprehensive, and sought-after media training, even by other services.

# FIVE TYPES OF MEDIA ENGAGEMENTS TO PREPARE FOR

These are the five types of media interviews to prepare for. Our Pentagon media training consisted of these different scenarios:

- Morning show
- Remote or talking head
- Man-on-the-street interview
- Combative interview
- Press conference

My executive at the Pentagon was well versed in space issues and needed the training to articulate new programs we hoped to fund and aid our warfighters. I prepared a fairly lengthy package of really tough questions I thought reporters might ask, along with drafted answers I'd created by working with space subject-matter experts. For this training, I provided this package not only to my executive but to a team of other professional communicators who role-played reporters. Those reporters used my questions as a guide and prepared additional questions. While this was stacking the deck against my executive, my team and I did so to create the most realistic training scenario in an academic space where the actual risk was minimal.

**Morning show:** We started off with the easiest of the interviews, the morning show. Our television newsroom is set much like you see on *Good Morning America*. This was not a contentious interview at all. The executive got comfortable on a set they'd never seen before talking to a reporter they'd never met. The reporter's demeanor was jovial and accommodating, the questions softball where everything goes very smoothly. We do this intentionally to build confidence in engaging with the press.

**Remote or talking head:** We then rolled into a remote interview, an increasingly common type today with so many people using Zoom and other online video platforms. This remote interview has its own challenges, primarily working technology, clear connectivity, crisp audio, and complementary video.

Ensure the background doesn't detract but enhances the message and you're set up with a good camera angle, level or even shot from slightly above the talent.

During the training, we deliberately planned for a technical difficulty where audio was severed for a short time, and the executive couldn't hear the question. Or the reporter acted as if their audio was unclear and asked the executive to repeat something they just said. This scenario forces the executives to think on their feet and maybe ask the reporter to repeat the question. All of this forces your principal to stay on message when they might otherwise become flustered.

**Man-on-the-street interview:** Next was a man-on-the-street interview where a reporter walks up to a person on the street and asks them a question with little, if any, warning. This scenario can also be contentious itself because it could lead to an ambush. This type of interview comes across as casual and undermines the person's authority as an expert. If they are just the man on the street, how can they really be an expert? I recommend avoiding this type of interview because it undermines the principal's authority as the expert. There are so many factors we can't control.

If you are approached by someone for a man-on-the-street interview, I would recommend you pause and say something to the effect of, "I'm not prepared to conduct this interview right now. Let's schedule something later." And stand your ground until the camera is off. If you walk away, you look like you have something to hide. If you do the interview and you're not prepared for what you want to say, it will be obvious.

**Combative interview:** The next interview was back in the studio and was like a *60 Minutes* exposé segment. The reporters didn't mince words and asked difficult questions about space control, a highly contentious issue, the cost of a specific program we were planning to add to the warfighters' arsenal, and personnel issues like recruiting and retaining members. It was clearly a combative interview intended to put our experts on the spot but conducted with the executive's best interest in mind.

**Press conference:** We finish off the training in a culminating press conference with multiple reporters rapidly firing questions on all possible topics. This forces the executive to call on reporters and handle switching from one topic to the other quickly. The interviewee has to stay on message and maintain their composure in a fairly intense setting.

After each media engagement type, we'd pause, and I'd have the camera operator roll the tape so we could view what had just transpired. I'd review the tape with the executive and that's when the lights would come on. The camera doesn't lie.

There is something about seeing yourself on video that truly makes an impression. There's no arguing with how you really presented the answers, how many "uhs" you uttered, and when you didn't answer the question at all. Reviewing the tape with the media trainer providing honest feedback helps your executive hone their public speaking skills.

Doing this training in an academic environment will better prepare them for when they have to do it in a real crisis.

Just like we did in the Pentagon, when I was stationed in Korea, public relations professionals participated in the exercise as reporters to add a sense of realism to the training. Each general officer, one from the United States and one from Korea, would make a statement. Then we'd open up for questions.

We identified an individual to serve as the facilitator, a role I often performed, much like a director on a movie set. I would call on reporters to ask probing questions and direct them at one general or another. We also identified someone to keep track of time so we would wrap up the press conference in a reasonable time.

Planners during the night shift prepared opening statements for the generals and likely questions and answers we would use the following day when we played out the press conference scenario. There were a lot of challenges with this type of scenario, chief among them the cultural differences and the language barrier.

While English was the primary language used, we would translate everything into Korean and allow for translation during the press conference. In an international setting, good translators were extremely valuable to effective communication. Translation also meant everything took twice as long. If you ever plan media training with an international partner, exercise patience and account for more time.

# THE REAL LEARNING OCCURS DURING THE AFTER-ACTION REVIEW

This exercise in media training included an after-action review immediately following the press conference. That is really where the greatest value in media training lies. The principals and their staff would go into another room where the team provided feedback on how each performed under pressure and what might need some polish.

In one such exercise, an executive answered a question totally off the mark and didn't include any of the key messages we'd discussed. In a diplomatic way, I provided feedback and an alternate way to deliver the answer and the key message and segue to another point to make.

The Korean translator was apparently appalled I would offer such direct and transparent feedback; he hesitated and asked his supervisor if he should even translate what I said. In Asian culture, respect for your elders and those appointed over you is of utmost importance. In my case, I was a lieutenant colonel, and the speaker was a general officer. My honest feedback, as diplomatically as I delivered it, was viewed by this translator as inappropriate feedback to provide.

While somewhat risky, it was my responsibility to help an executive refine their communication and delivery method to make them a better public speaker in crisis. Providing honest feedback helps your CEO or president improve their communication skills and is an important element of your job. Conducting training like this in an exercise environment is a safe space where learning can take place before the cameras are rolling for real.

## WHAT YOU NEED TO KNOW

- Strive to understand all you can about your mission and organizational values so you can better articulate it to the media when a crisis hits.
- Have the courage to ask questions and find problems needing a fix before they become a public crisis. Ensure you have a working knowledge of your business practices, policies, and processes in place, and when you speak up, you solidify your value to the organization.
- Your principals must have the finesse and wherewithal to work through technical problems and overcome a live situation when technology goes wrong. Provide media training where the technology fails so your president or CEO can practice overcoming it before it happens on live television.
- Mitigating language barriers takes patience and more time. Invest time now preparing for a crisis and secure a qualified translator you trust.

- To better plan for your next crisis, conduct media training for your leadership team. Put them through the traps with a likely business scenario gone wrong so they can practice being in the hot seat before the cameras are rolling for real.
- Offer candor, diplomacy, and honesty to help your leadership team be more effective crisis communicators.

## CASE STUDY: OPERATION VARSITY BLUES

### The Setup

Four University of Southern California (USC) staffers were implicated in Operation Varsity Blues, which is being called the largest-ever admissions bribery case prosecuted by the US Department of Justice. Among those at USC were senior associate athletic director Donna Heinel, ex-women's soccer coach Ali Khosroshahin, ex-assistant soccer coach Laura Janke, and men's and women's water polo coach Jovan Vavic.

According to charging documents, the USC sports staffers named would, in exchange for large financial gifts, designate students as recruited athletes, even if they didn't play sports so the academic standards for admission would be lower. They fell prey to the same scheme Jorge Salcedo, former UCLA men's soccer coach, did when he was sentenced to eight months behind bars for pocketing $200,000 in bribes to help applicants get into UCLA as bogus athletic recruits.

William Rick Singer allegedly organized the scheme and received bribes totaling $25 million from parents between 2011 and 2018 to guarantee their children's admission to elite schools. Some students were admitted with doctored test scores, others by photoshopped pictures depicting nonexistent athletic prowess. Singer paid off multiple athletic department employees and false test takers to guide kids in through what he dubbed his "side door."

**The Response**

Negative coverage for more than a year.

USC put up a one-page Frequently Asked Questions (FAQs) outlining their new process for athletics admission with a link to their core values. Really? There was a change in leadership within the athletic department but not with the university president.

Media coverage showed many famous, wealthy clients including actresses Lori Loughlin and Felicity Huffman walking into judicial courts backed up by B-roll of red-carpet events with their kids.

**The Result**

The nationwide scandal led to charges against more than fifty people, including thirty-five wealthy parents who prosecutors say paid bribes totaling up to $6.5 million to have their children accepted into elite US colleges like USC, Yale, Stanford, and Georgetown. Bribes were often in the form of donations to the universities and facilitated by scam ringleader Singer, owner of a college counseling service called Key Worldwide Foundation and Edge College & Career Network.

## My Take

There's not much evidence of active engagement from USC leadership in handling the crisis. I was able to find a series of YouTube videos with holiday messages but nothing from President Carol L. Folt on the scandal. There was no apology or assurance those involved in the scam would be dealt with appropriately.

USC should have leveraged every available opportunity to showcase what they were doing instead of hiding behind the FAQs. Folt could have made public statements at key points to protect their brand. What could have been a one- or two-day story dragged out for months in the press while the investigation was taking place. Meanwhile, USC and other universities offered little about their commitment to honesty and integrity.

Singer ultimately ended up cooperating with the DOJ to bring down those he'd recruited and parents he'd accepted payments from.

USC instituted a number of changes to its recruiting process—a series of checks and balances to prevent such unethical procedures from occurring again. Despite these changes, their brand has been tarnished.

# MEDIA TRAINING

Here's a fact: Brilliant business people, CEOs, and company presidents are not necessarily effective communicators. Providing realistic media training ahead of a real crisis is a must for your senior executives. Doing so ahead of a crisis provides a safe and controlled environment to practice in and will pay off in spades when a crisis really occurs.

If you would like to take the initial step toward developing meaningful media training for your organization, email me at *angela@TheViragoCircle.com* or contact me through my website *www.TheViragoCircle.com*.

I have conducted a ninety-minute crisis media training session for countless executives in and outside of the military. If your leadership team needs a deep dive that includes all scenarios, we can develop those ahead of a crisis taking place so you are ready to go when one does. And believe me, it will, sooner or later.

# 5

# WHEN "NO COMMENT" JUST WON'T WORK: HOW TO BUILD PROFESSIONAL RELATIONSHIPS WITH REPORTERS

**W**e in the communication office received a call from the command post at Elmendorf Air Force Base, near Anchorage, Alaska, that a military member had brandished a weapon in the hospital and was threatening to take their own life. In the instant we received the call, my public affairs team switched to crisis mode.

I could feel my heart racing inside my chest as the different scenarios played out in my head. I rushed to the command post to get a handle on what was taking place. We began gathering facts, and I conveyed them to my team, along with direction and guidance on what to do next. When I arrived at the command post, I was met by the vice wing commander and other leaders. He was in contact with the hospital commander. Communication lines were open and facts began to materialize.

- Early reports indicated shots were fired. Were they?
- Where specifically in the hospital was the individual?
- What patients were nearby, if any?
- How did security forces respond?
- What type of mental state was the individual in?
- What would happen to the shooter?
- Were they receiving mental health counseling?
- How about those affected by this incident?

It didn't take long for the press to find out there was a situation developing at the hospital. My chief of media began fielding calls almost immediately. She automatically knew to log in the time of their calls, and their affiliate, making note of contact information and what their specific questions were. While there were only three major television stations in Anchorage, all three called to inquire as to what was unfolding. I developed a holding statement with a promise to return calls as soon as there was any verifiable information. The holding statement was little more than "I'll look into the situation and get back with you."

Next, based on what we knew, my media relations chief began drafting a press release to include the who, what, where, when, and why. Once I verified the release with the command post, I had her distribute it to the press. Because of the high-tech equipment and resources on our military installation, Elmendorf, like most military bases, is not open to the public. I then notified our security forces that reporters would be at our front gate to film their stand-ups for the evening news, using our gate in the background.

Since the day presented a crisis, it was all hands on deck as my team actively managed the information flow. Everything else planned went out the window. This is very important for you, your team, and your leadership to understand and embrace. You must actively engage, gather, and verify the information with your reliable sources. Without a factual press statement, the media may have gotten the story completely wrong and used much more inflammatory language. They may have created a false narrative altogether—certainly something I did not want.

The first coverage appeared on the 5:00 p.m. news, followed by an update at 6:00 p.m., then again at 10:00 p.m. The reporter used the information provided in the release and the reporter's stand-up filmed outside the gate indicated the Air Force was actively handling the situation. I made my commander aware of the coverage received. While dramatic, it was factual. The base leadership was represented fairly as actively managing the situation, and reports included accurate information my team had provided.

When you engage with the media, especially during a crisis, everything in your background as a subject-matter or brand expert culminates in how effectively you communicate. Before a crisis occurs, it's important to establish a level of transparency and be responsive to media requests. Plan events and invite press to cover them. Provide access to your president or CEO. Do what you can to support the media's unquenchable thirst for information.

When this active shooter situation presented itself, the media knew precisely the office and person to call. My team had already established a working relationship with them. They knew we would release information to them as quickly as possible.

Most people avoid engaging with reporters for fear of being misquoted or having their comments taken out of context. Ignoring the press or the crisis provides zero opportunity to explain what happened and what you are doing to keep misinformation from occurring again. Engaging with the press provides the opportunity to control the narrative and protect your brand.

As a crisis communicator, you should be a part of the leadership team and work directly for the commander, CEO, or president. You have to think strategically and holistically about each potential crisis. You may even have to convince some on the team that being forthcoming and transparent will help you weather the storm.

So it's critical to establish rapport, trust, and confidence with your boss ahead of any crisis once it hits. If you are not in the inner circle, you may be left out with an aftermath tarnishing your reputable brand. In the situation I described with the active shooter, if my leadership didn't know and trust me, it would have been far more difficult to gather and verify the facts and make that initial release.

Know there are processes you can put in place ahead of a crisis and some organizational elements you can establish today to help you better manage your next crisis. I provide a pre-crisis checklist you can use ahead of a crisis as an easy reference below.

## PRE-CRISIS CHECKLIST

**Here are actions you can take TODAY to help you manage your next crisis.**

- Ensure you have a list of people on your leadership team like the CEO, COO, legal, public relations/ corporate communication, human resources, and finance. Add others you think are appropriate such as research and development, head of manufacturing, and safety director.

- Assemble a recall list of your key communicators during crisis. Think web developer, photographer, videographer, and writer. Identify their roles so each has an understanding of who they will work with.
- Establish relationships with the local, regional, and federal government agencies that help you perform your mission or partners who help you conduct your business.
- Establish relationships with the local press so you know them ahead of a crisis taking place. Make sure they know who you are and call you with questions.
- Determine who will serve as the on-scene commander. It's likely your chief operations officer or operations chief. This will be the person who is managing the crash site of a downed aircraft or mass shooter. Establish rapport with them early on. They will be invaluable as you ascertain the most accurate information as soon as possible and release it.
- Establish other key members you will likely work with during a crisis. In addition to you, the communication/public relations team leader, add the attorney and key subject-matter experts, depending on the type of crisis you are dealing with.
- Update your website and post information on your social media platforms regularly to establish transparency in your product or mission.

# BUILDING MEDIA RELATIONS

Building media relations is a process that takes time and attention. Like any other relationship, these liaisons are not built overnight. Two positions I held that were heavy on media relations were while I was in Afghanistan and when I was at the Pentagon. While both were very different environments, the common elements included gaining familiarity with someone ahead of a crisis so you already have an established relationship when a crisis hits.

Typically, reporters have a beat they cover so they can provide more comprehensive coverage for their bureau or news agency. Know the press who cover your beat and get to know them through the articles they write and that are published or reported.

A tactic I successfully employed when I was in Kabul, Afghanistan, was to meet with reporters for afternoon tea at the British cantina on base. It was not an on-the-record conversation but more a way to provide context to current operations. I prefaced the meeting with that very statement: "This is an off-the-record conversation, not for quote."

I would ask reporters what stories they were working on and what approach they were taking. I'd provide them with information to help them understand what combat operations were like and the conditions our troops were operating under. I might suggest someone who would deliver a good interview or connect the reporter with another public affairs officer to set up an interview at another location.

Investing time getting to know the reporters who cover your organization is a way to successfully shape the story without being quoted.

I developed a comfortable relationship with numerous reporters while at the Pentagon. I would talk to reporters frequently outside of official media interviews—not on the record but as a friendly conversation to better understand the topics they were interested in, what was on their minds, and their impressions of where the story was.

A dozen or more reporters covered the military space beat. They were transparent with their story angle, which allowed me to better prepare my experts for the interview. Those same reporters knew I would provide ample access to my principals, and I would respond by deadline.

The more you can do to help the press gain access to your experts, the greater the chance the coverage will be factually correct. Done consistently over time, getting access and being responsive helped shape coverage we received on space programs.

While a quick Google search may provide some information about a reporter, the value of holding a genuine conversation with the press cannot be understated. Here are some questions you can pose to start building those relationships:

- Where are you from originally?
- How'd you get into the news business?

- How long have you been with your agency?
- What industry topics do you find most interesting?
- Are there other reporters you collaborate with on stories?
- Which particular story are you most proud of or which was most interesting for you to cover?

These kinds of questions provide insight as to how reporters approach their business and better inform you as you set up interviews.

Before setting up an interview, ask the press a few questions so you know what you're getting into:

- Who else are you talking to about this partic-ular topic?
- What are you learning about the topic?
- Scope the interview. Ask them what questions they have of your CEO or expert. While they may not divulge the specific questions, they should at least provide areas they'd like to cover.
- Ask them what their angle is or what perspec-tive they are writing from.
- There are deadlines, and then there are "no kidding deadlines." Know for sure the latest day and time you could arrange an interview or provide a statement to affect the story.
- Time is valuable to your experts and report-ers. Set a time limit for the interview and honor it.

It's challenging in today's information overload environment to read every piece of news every single day. Focus on your industry and the reporters who typically cover your company. When you see an interesting piece you learned something from, send them a quick note to let them know the article was well written or beneficial to the public.

I did this when I was stationed at the Pentagon, and it created an amiable working relationship with the press. I would pitch story ideas to reporters ahead of time. This gives the reporters a heads-up on the topics covered so they could better prepare their questions. I keep reporters' phone numbers and emails in my contacts so I can directly pitch story ideas and personally invite them to cover public events.

# THE POWER OF NEGOTIATION

Negotiating the parameters of any media engagement is important to manage expectations and shape the outcome of the story. Everyone likes to know the rules of any game ahead of time. Asking a few simple yet direct questions to set the scope of the interaction ensures the best possible outcome for engaging with the press.

**Assume *everything* you say is on the record and the press is recording, unless you negotiate otherwise.** When they are conducting a one-on-one interview, there are a number of ways you or your experts may be quoted. Negotiating this is important ahead of time so the reporter has a clear understanding of how they are using the information. You may be quoted by name and title, as a company or agency spokesperson, or as someone familiar with the organization. For comprehensive ways you can be quoted, see Your Guide to Being Attributed on the folllowing page.

Include a time limit when setting up an interview and adhere to the guidelines. Understand the reporter's deadline and treat the time crunch seriously. If you can't meet a deadline, tell the reporter as soon as possible. You may also have to be assertive with your leadership to make an interview a priority within the reporter's time constraints so you can impact their coverage.

- Consider the news agency you are engaging with ahead of setting up the interview. Even though every news agency does not carry the weight of the *Washington Post*, they deserve professional respect.
- Who owns the newspaper, television station, or web platform?
- What is their editorial slant, if any?
- What else has your journalist written about you and the topic in the past?
- Who else have they talked to about this particular story?

The answers to these questions arm you with valuable information and aid you in mitigating the risk associated with any media interview, especially during a crisis. Know and understand there is always a risk when engaging with any reporter. The risk of not engaging is typically far greater.

When you talk to reporters or set up an interview with your principal, knowing how you will be quoted is almost as important as what you say. When I was at the Pentagon, I worked with a number of national and international reporters who know a lot about our space operations.

In one instance, I provided a statement on one of our space programs to one particular *Wall Street Journal* reporter. I assumed I would be quoted and on the record with my name and rank. They did not attribute it to me personally but as "a military officer familiar with the program." I took exception to this because I had researched the information extensively, knew it was accurate and carefully crafted the language before releasing it. When the *Wall Street Journal* attributed it as they did, it gave their readership the impression the Air Force had something to hide, that someone would only provide this information if they weren't quoted by name.

I called the reporter after the story ran and told her I took exception to how she attributed the information. Essentially, she said, this is how we do it in the journal. In other words, the information was more important than who it was attributed to. It was my mistake as I failed to negotiate this ahead of the exchange. For every exchange she and I had after that, I made sure we both understood precisely how the information would be attributed.

Before your next one-on-one interview, think about how you and your comments will be characterized. Negotiate with the reporter ahead of the exchange. Once the ground rules are established, set up the interview and choose your words carefully.

## YOUR GUIDE TO BEING ATTRIBUTED

Before your next one-on-one interview, think about how you will be attributed and negotiate that with the reporter ahead of the exchange. These are some of the more common attributions for a one-on-one interaction I've used:

- **On the record** as Angela Billings, Lieutenant Colonel, United States Air Force. This is the most common attribution: name, position or rank, and company affiliation the press will use and is your default for an official comment. During my deployment to Afghanistan, my rank stayed the same but I was then serving as NATO Spokesperson Lt. Col. Angela Billings. This was my default attribution for any combat-related facts. The branch of service or country I was from was not used.
- **On the record simply as a spokesperson** is almost on par with the above and still holds weight even though your name isn't used. I have used this type of attribution to place more emphasis on the fact itself.
- **On background** as a senior military officer. Sometimes, leaving your name out is best. The reporter uses the information and the reader knows it has merit but without a name attached. There are

occasions when a degree of ambiguity is better when you simply want to establish a fact and the reporter already has corroborating information.

- **Deep background**, not to quote you directly but for context and an opportunity to guide a reporter in the right direction. Doing a deep background interview forces the reporter to find someone else to go on the record.

- **Off the record** to distance yourself from whatever the reporter was writing about but when you make the judgment it's important the reporter has the information. There have been times during an on-the-record interview I or my principal have stopped the recording and provided information off the record. This is usually when you have a sense the reporter is going off on a tangent or drawing factually incorrect conclusions and you hope to steer them back on track.

- **No comment**, which I rarely recommend. If you respond with "no comment," reporters will go elsewhere to find information, any information. The reporter may have inaccurate information from someone outside the loop or maybe even from your competition. If I was unable to provide a substantive comment, I would often direct a reporter to a certain organization or person who may provide a better or more complete perspective. Many reporters aren't necessarily a fan of this tactic as they may take it as you giving them the runaround, but used judiciously, this strategy can pay off.

# PREPARE FOR THE INTERVIEW

Approach the interview as a strategic opportunity and have a clear idea of what you want to convey before you sit down with the reporter. Consider providing numbers, data, or supporting analysis. I've found the more research you do for the reporter, the more accurate the reporting is.

Prepare, practice, and rehearse what you will say. Practicing the delivery of your main points and how you will answer the tough questions is paramount to nailing the interview, presenting your best self and preserving your business brand. Brainstorming the tough questions and answers with other communication professionals on my team is the most effective way to prepare myself, the commander, or CEO for the dynamic environment a press interview brings.

If time allows, when you schedule an interview, schedule the prep session the day ahead or even a few hours before the interview to allow this rehearsal.

Don't leave anything to chance and plan the logistics ahead of time to ensure things go smoothly. Will it be a phone, Zoom, or remote television interview? Make sure you have the location with the address. If it's on the phone, determine who will call whom and on what line. Make sure both parties have each other's contact information.

If you are taking your CEO or boss to a television or radio station, go yourself the day before. Get a feel for the layout, the set, whether you will be sitting or standing. If you are sitting, ask the reporter for a chair that does not swivel. For a radio interview, make sure your boss understands they will be wearing a headset and speaking into a microphone for the best audio. The more information you can determine ahead of time will alleviate some of the stress.

When faced with a crisis, it's important to understand you always have the option of doing or saying nothing. If you choose not to engage, understand somebody else may be telling your story instead of you. It's always a judgment call. But this underscores why it's important to have an established rapport with the leadership in your organization so you are included in the conversations and advising them on when to engage with the press and what to say publicly.

A crisis is where risk meets opportunity. Understand there is always risk involved when you talk to the media. Once the words leave your mouth, you can't take them back. Each interview is an opportunity to tell your story. The risk of not engaging is far greater. If you don't tell your story, reporters will go elsewhere for answers to their questions. I assert it is far better to engage at the first opportunity to mitigate the risk of factually incorrect coverage.

# EMBARGOED INFORMATION

When you embargo information, you provide the information to a reporter or reporters in advance of the release date. The embargoed press release or interview is shared ahead of the agreed release date and time. Unlike standard news releases, which typically have FOR IMMEDIATE RELEASE on them, the embargoed release states the future date and time the information can be used.

Media are expected to use the information in creating their story but not post it one minute before. This more sophisticated approach gives reporters additional time to write a more in-depth article or package in an extensive piece. Releasing embargoed information is a strategy typically reserved for technical topics or those involving multiple stakeholders so everyone can agree on the releasable information.

When I worked for a research university, we used this strategy to release a significant development in spinal cord research so that we could garner the most in-depth coverage on the day the research was made public.

Agreeing to embargo information involves great trust as the media will have the information well before the release date—sometimes even weeks. The inherent risk in presenting information to reporters ahead of time is they may simply disregard the agreement. When I've worked with reporters on embargoed information, I've not experienced that. The reporter's name and reputation are on the line, and most appreciate the additional time to prepare more comprehensive coverage.

Though this delayed release technique is not typically used in times of crisis, as you think through developing professional relationships with the press, you can leverage the offer of embargoed information so you garner more comprehensive coverage.

This chapter includes steps you can do today to enhance your media relations with the press, ultimately helping you better manage your next crisis. Take a look at my crisis checklist, and if you haven't already, implement those items right way.

## CRISIS CHECKLIST

Once you know you're in crisis, take these actions:

- **Establish what you know and what facts must be determined.** Ask questions and go find the answers to help the leadership team manage the crisis.
- **Inform your internal team and stakeholders.** Email or text is likely the most expedient way to make your team aware of the situation. Provide regular updates as more information becomes available.
- **Call your board and inform them of the crisis.** Depending on the nature of the crisis, you may consider calling a special board meeting to deliver the information in person or via Zoom. Provide them with as much information as you know and rely on them to help you avoid pitfalls.
- **Coordinate with the local government agencies as needed.**
- **Prepare the most likely Q&As to help your leadership/spokesperson be prepared.** These will turn into an FAQ on your social platforms and website.

- **Write your initial press release.** Include the most basic of information: who, what, when, where, why, and how. You may not know the why or how initially, but don't let the uncertainty keep you from being transparent. You may feel the urge to speculate about the why and how, but don't. Reserve comment on the why and the how for a follow-up release as more details become available.
- **Establish who will field and track media calls.** Establish a tracking mechanism to follow up with reporters individually. Point them to your website or invite them to the press conference.
- **Prepare follow-up releases and make public statements when you have significant information to release.**
- **Depending on the magnitude and scope of your crisis, consider holding a press conference.**

# WHAT YOU NEED TO KNOW

- Spend time with your CEO or president and other members of your leadership team to understand your lines of business. When a public crisis threatens to negatively impact your business, you will have that established trust and be a part of the team that solves the problem.
- Give your team structure with assigned roles ahead of a crisis so you can respond quickly once it occurs.

- Transparency—having an up-to-date website and an active social media presence—is now the foundational practice for just about any brand. Leverage these built-in platforms ahead of a crisis with accurate, readily available information so people know who you are before a crisis shines a spotlight on you.
- Establish relationships with the press as you do with anyone else you work with regularly. Understand the media cycle and help your reporters be their best by meeting deadlines. Take deadlines seriously and emphasize to your leadership and subject-matter experts the importance of providing timely information or access.
- For any press engagement, do research ahead of any interview and set ground rules and time limits so everyone has clear expectations. State the ground rules plainly so everyone knows who is speaking, their titles, and how they will be attributed in any coverage.

## CASE STUDY: ABBOTT NUTRITION

### The Setup

You may recall the nationwide baby formula shortage in the spring of 2022. Abbott Nutrition, a major formula supplier, issued a recall and closed their Sturgis, Michigan, manufacturing plant when the bacteria, *cronobacter sakazakii*, was discovered. A whistleblower first drew attention to poor plant conditions in October 2021. But the US Food and Drug Administration (FDA) didn't interview the whistleblower until December and didn't reinspect the plant until late January, attributing in-person inspection delays to the COVID-19 pandemic.

Abbott boasted a 40 percent market share of the United States baby formula before the plant closure.

**The Response**
- Late.
- There was no sense of urgency after the whistleblower made their claims of unsafe business practices.
- While the contaminant was found in the nonproduct contact areas, the plant was shut down for inspection.

**The Result**
- Negative.
- The baby formula pseudo-monopoly really created the crisis and should never have been allowed to exist.
- The global pandemic and subsequent business closures created supply chain problems, which severely impacted an already vulnerable market segment, primarily lower-income minority families relying on the federal Women, Infants and Children (WIC) program to receive formula.
- Abbott Nutrition exhibited no sense of urgency to uncover or correct the safety problems and displayed no accountability with their leadership.

- Outside of a single news release on their website dated February 17, they only provided phone numbers and links to other websites to the barrage of social media posts on their Facebook page.
- The FDA investigated and was very broad in identifying the "themes of issues" causing the crisis: a need for better information technology systems to track and exchange data, more staffing and training, an updated emergency response system to deal with food safety crises in real time, which has long been a criticism of the agency.

## The Result

- The crisis brought the existence of a near-monopoly by less than a handful of US baby formula manufacturers to the forefront.
- The shortage exposed limits placed on foreign suppliers despite their adherence to tough FDA standards. There was no conclusive evidence any infant deaths could be directly attributed to the carcinogen.

## My Take

When the whistleblower first suspected contamination, Abbott should have suspended production immediately, and the FDA should have dispatched inspectors right away. Abbott should have taken ownership of the crisis immediately and issued public statements to that effect. If they had, it's quite possible they would have contained the bacteria inside the facility, which would have allowed the plant to remain open.

This immediate response may have avoided a nationwide crisis altogether. Abbott's leadership should have held a press conference stating what they suspected and began a recall then, not months later. Abbott should have made regular public statements and updates across social media channels, not referred consumers to other agencies. As Tylenol did, Abbott should have provided a refund of any suspected contaminated product.

Once on site, the FDA should have had a greater sense of urgency and issued their report immediately, making a clear statement about the plant's cleanliness and the way forward. Abbott's poor process identified by the whistleblower points toward a needed culture change inside the company. Clearly, there was no cohesive communication strategy from Abbott or the FDA.

The FDA report was first issued by FDA Commissioner Robert Califf months after his initial refusal to answer congressional questions in May 2022, citing the ongoing internal investigation. The US eventually loosened restrictions on foreign manufacturers and involved the US military to bring supplies to the states.

Months after the crisis has seemingly subsided, the developmental delays babies under one year old without needed formula will experience is unknown. The fear and desperation of new mothers searching frantically for formula during a critical developmental time in their child's life were significant.

# 6

# IS THIS A CRISIS? YES OR NO

How do you know you have a crisis on your hands? Is it a sixth sense or are there accepted barometers for going from your standard engagement with your customers or clients and switching gears into crisis mode? Let me walk you through my own crisis decision matrix to identify when you may be experiencing your next crisis and what actions you may need to take next.

I was at Elmendorf Air Force Base in Anchorage, Alaska, when the Department of Defense determined every service member would receive the anthrax vaccine. This policy was a direct reaction to the suspicion Saddam Hussein had chemical weapons stored to use against his adversaries. The anthrax vaccine was developed to protect service members against this possible chemical weapons exposure. Since this was across every service, the Department of Defense provided the policy and guidance from Washington, DC, and the individual services had to implement the policy at the local level.

I worked with the hospital commander and public health officials to provide factual information about what the vaccine would protect against and the possible side effects. These side effects were primarily a deep soreness in the arm, and, typically, the second shot wasn't as painful as the first. After the initial shot, service members would return six weeks later to receive their booster.

Much like the United States managed the COVID-19 vaccine for the entire population, the Department of Defense had already done so for anthrax decades before.

Some service members took exception to receiving the vaccine, which effectively ended their military careers. I worked closely with the judge advocate general on the process for separating service members. The DOD, the Air Force, and every military base had to manage the departure of otherwise qualified individuals from military service, thus creating a force development crisis in recruiting that HR would have to contend with. The mandatory vaccine created a crisis (refusal of the vaccine) that created another crisis (difficulty recruiting new members).

My team had to communicate with our internal audience—service members and their commanders—about the process by which people would be separated from the military. We used our base newspaper to convey the process for separating from the military and set up commanders' calls or town hall meetings.

The possible negative impact on women's fertility was a common reason women refused the vaccine. Some service members would talk to the press about their separation. When reporters called me about specific individuals, the Health Insurance Portability and Accountability Act (HIPAA) prevented me from revealing any personal health information about any specific person. I had DOD talking points and focused on what I could say about why the vaccine was needed and the process to protect the Air Force and DOD brand.

To maintain transparency, I set up interviews with medical doctors, the base attorney, and commanders of people who refused the vaccine.

My communication team was already engaging with our audience—service members and their families—about the change in policy and the impact on them.

You and your company, agency, or brand are likely managing all or most of these platforms and promoting your business or your brand in similar ways:

- Website presence with great content
- Regular engagement with your internal stakeholders or team members
- Social media engagement including platforms like Twitter, Facebook, and Instagram
- Writing for your blog or publishing other regularly scheduled online content
- Writing press releases
- Preparing your CEO or president for speaking engagements including conducting research, drafting bullet points, and providing logistics for the event
- Promoting events and inviting the press to cover them
- Planned board interaction with your stakeholders or stockholders
- Individual interactions promoting your product or brand

- Planning sessions for the next week, month, quarter, and year

These engagements are your steady-state or day-to-day communication with your audiences. In a crisis, we shift from the day-to-day operations and implement a concerted communication strategy. So far in this book, I have spent time addressing actions you can take ahead of a crisis to better position yourself to manage through it. So how do you determine if you're actually facing a crisis?

# ASK QUESTIONS

Crisis may be born out of many wayward happenings. While my experience includes airplane crashes and troops in combat, yours may involve leadership errors in judgment or product malfunctions. Asking key questions of your leadership team will help you and your CEO or president analyze the magnitude of what's in front of you and determine what actions you need to take to actively manage the situation.

I've compiled a list of questions you should ask, and if the answer is yes, you may have a crisis of some magnitude on your hands.

- Was there a death or serious bodily injury?
- Is there additional risk to safety, public health, or life?
- Is an apology or condolences appropriate?

- Was there an ethics violation?
- Have you broken any laws or regulations?
- Do you have any legal obligation requiring public explanation?
- Are you morally bound to share the information publicly?
- Is a product you manufacture faulty and a danger to your consumers?
- Are there suspicious or untoward HR practices involved?

During a crisis, you, as a professional communicator, provide immense value to your boss. No one else in the organization is in the specific situation you are with quite the perspective you have. By posing tough questions, whether individually with your boss or privately with a small leadership team, you add value through the crisis.

The answers to these questions will direct your next steps to protecting your brand and your business. You and the entire team will have to make the judgment call as to the next right steps to take. You will be key to determining the words to convey what those actions are. Articulating what the situation is, what you are doing to mitigate it and keep it from happening in the future requires your full attention.

Consider who your primary audiences are. First and foremost, you must inform your internal team as to the crisis taking place. These include your employees, stakeholders and stockholders, and board members. This is critical as these people will be the coalition who will band with you through the crisis. Keep them informed so they will echo the same points you state officially to their network, friends, and family. Email is likely the most intuitive way to reach your audience directly, but your company may use videos, have an employee portal, or use several available apps to stay connected.

You may consider a number of tactics to convey what your crisis is and what you are doing about it. The main point is whatever you are *saying* you are *doing* has to match what you are *actually doing.*

- Is your leadership taking accountability and making changes because of some deficiency in practice or policy?
- Is there an apology due or a remedy for what has transpired?
- Do you have a glitch in your process needing refinement or an improvement you must implement?
- What are your lessons learned through this crisis?
- How are you going to mitigate the possibility of this ever happening again?

Having an active social media presence—whether on one, some, or all of the available platforms—is now fundamental to any successful business. And it's important your boss or CEO allows you the latitude to manage information on these platforms. Keep key people informed about the comments and questions you receive through social media. You will take the information you glean via social and take it to the team. That information is invaluable on how you will proceed.

Once it becomes clear your crisis is on a scale requiring a public statement, thinking through your delivery ahead of time will alleviate some of the stress. Just like scaling a business, you often must scale in crisis. Perhaps you begin with a holding statement until you have more facts. Send out a press release. If things deteriorate, then plan your full-on press conference. This graduated response demonstrates your aware-ness and active engagement to managing the crisis.

## CRISIS PRESS CONFERENCE

Once you are in full crisis mode and the demand for more information warrants it, a press conference is typically the best way to release all the information in one fell swoop. You are likely to have twenty-four hours or less to execute, so mentally walking through a press event ahead of time will help ensure a suc-cessful one.

In the military, before engaging with the enemy we always conduct reconnaissance. This is when you check out the operating environment and look at the terrain. Determine where the high ground is so you have a more complete picture and identify potentially vulnerable areas to avoid. Apply this same approach when plan-ning and executing a successful press conference.

These are the steps I take when planning a crisis press conference.

- **Location:** Determine the best location for the press conference. Visit the venue ahead of time if you can to make sure it is easily accessible and aesthetically pleasing. Familiarizing yourself with the venue beforehand alleviates some of the unknown questions your leadership has and the stress of planning for it. If you are setting it up in a remote location, check that you have internet connectivity.

- **Spokesperson:** Determine who your spokesperson is. While it is likely to be your senior executive or board member, sometimes starting at the top is not the right route to take. Talk through the type of crisis you are experiencing with your leadership team and determine who should be behind the microphone.

- **Run of show:** Develop a run of show or an agenda, a cue card mapping out the order of things: where you are, who will speak first, how long the event will be, how you will wrap things up. Provide this to your speakers and anyone else involved in the execution of the press conference, and include your tech person.

- **Opening statement:** Prepare your opening statement with the facts as you know them. Use vernacular you find most comfortable. If the language is not what you typically use, you will stutter, stammer, and lose your composure, which will detract from your message. A strong opening statement commands attention and establishes the tone. Print it in a font large enough to comfortably read from. Number your pages so if the order is misplaced, the statement is easily reassembled. Put the statement in a folder or binder with the speaker's name on the front. Don't staple it as flipping through pages looks awkward for your speaker when he or she is behind the podium and is distracting to the audience. Make an extra hard copy of the statement for yourself, just in case something happens to theirs on the way to the press conference and have it handy, or if something happens to them and you have to deliver the comments for them.

- **Visual aids:** Determine if you need some sort of visual aid like a PowerPoint presentation or another display to depict what has transpired. If you do use this to reinforce what you have to say, make it large enough to see from the back of the room and post it on your website after the press conference concludes.
- **Handouts:** If you have a handout for the press, prepare it ahead of time and hang the information on your web page once the press conference is over.
- **Posture:** Decide if you or your main spokesperson will be standing or sitting. Standing portrays more authority, and if you go this

route, you'll also need a microphone and podium for the spokesperson to place their notes on.

- **Set the stage:** Commonly called a "step and repeat," use a backdrop with your company logo on it, as well as a logo placard affixed to the front of the podium subtly tells the world who you are. Consider including a national, state, or other flag as they provide a boundary that flanks your speaker and centers your audience's attention.

- **Microphone:** Will you have a lavalier mic (one your spokesperson wears on their lapel) or not? Someone needs to have a handle on the technology, and if you don't do it yourself, identify a reliable source on site who will manage audio. If you are wearing a mic or anywhere near one, always assume the mic is hot. Anything you say, even in whispered tones, may be heard and is, therefore, attributable to you.

- **Likely Q&A:** Have you reviewed the toughest questions you are likely to be asked and rehearsed your answers? Have you media trained your key speakers? Your team should be able to help think through the best answers. There will always be questions you don't have the answers to right away and saying "I don't know" is certainly acceptable. Given your situation, it may be appropriate to commit to researching information or releasing it once it is available. Be careful here and ensure you know if there are legal or personal privacy limits.

The standard questions you anticipate addressing during the press conference, regardless of the crisis, will revolve around the five Ws and H: who, what, when, where, why, and how, plus the big question, what are you doing to correct or remedy the situation?

- Who is involved?
- What happened?
- When did this take place?
- Where did this occur?
- Why did this happen?
- How did this happen?
- What are you doing to correct or remedy the situation?

Part of your job is to help your president or CEO think through the answers to these questions, identify the right next steps, and prepare them for the onslaught of questions they will receive. Anxiety and stress will be high, and admitting your company or a trusted individual inside the company has made a terrible mistake is a hard pill to swallow.

The most important point to remember in this chapter is whatever you say has to match what you are actually doing. Any company can apologize for a wrongdoing, but if they are not taking active steps to correct the situation that created the crisis in the first place, no words can make it right. Facts are facts and conveying them honestly is always your best bet.

I learned early in my career, when presented with a potential crisis situation, there is always the option to do nothing. I attended a Public Relations Society of America conference and Jim Lukaszewski, America's Crisis Guru®, was presenting on crisis communication. The room was packed and there were PR professionals like myself lining the walls and sitting on the floor to hear him talk about how he has helped his clients manage through crisis.

Lukaszewski said quite simply, you always have the option of doing nothing. I've offered that as an option ever since. While doing or saying nothing is clearly an option, there is always an inherent risk involved. If you don't engage, someone else may step in and fill the void you've created. They are likely to have their own opinion and they may not have all the facts.

With your company's good name and reputation on the line, inaction may result in lost credibility, your brand may suffer, and you may alienate clients or lose customers. You and your leadership team must stay engaged, ask tough questions, and weigh the risk of doing nothing, saying nothing, against the benefit of owning up to the crisis.

While you're not likely to flawlessly walk through a crisis without mistakes or missteps, the tools I've provided here will help you manage through it. You will survive and live to see another day. You may even find you thrive on the adrenaline that comes from the crisis.

Check out my press conference checklist for a quick reference on planning the best one possible in the short amount of time you'll have. You can also find my crisis decision matrix at the end of this chapter and use it as a prompt for your company's action.

As the crisis subsides and you transition to post-crisis, you may find it beneficial to conduct specific one-on-one interviews with targeted media outlets or submit an Op-Ed to a specific newspaper your key audience subscribes to. Both of these approaches demonstrate a thoughtful follow-up to convey what actions you have taken to remedy the situation and present a closure to the crisis.

## CRISIS PRESS CONFERENCE CHECKLIST

If you only have twenty-four hours to plan, twenty-four hours is all the time it will take.

- **Choose a location and coordinate with anyone who's important for access to your press event.** For the military, since most events were on a secure installation, coordinate with whoever is in charge of security, the military police. For those operating in the free world, look to local law enforcement and local city officials for needed permits and access from whoever owns the building.
- **Stage the press event.** Determine the physical needs of the press conference: podium, table, background, seating, microphone, and any other technology that will deliver clear sound and audio.

- **Determine who your spokesperson is.** While it's likely your senior executive or board member will be the spokesperson, there are some times when starting at the top is not the right route to take. Be thoughtful about who the right person is.
- **Send out a press advisory in advance.** Include all of your pertinent information: when and where the press should show up, what they will be witnessing, whom they will be hearing from, and any other facts about your product or the mission.
- **Credential your media.** Be sure the representative is a legitimate reporter and affiliated with a press organization. If they are a freelancer, they are likely on contract with a publication so you can ask them for a letter of intent or reach out to the publication directly to verify.
- **Prepare media packets ahead of time.** Items to include are fact sheets about your product or mission and biographical data on your key speakers. Supporting facts and figures are always great as they lend credence to what you are saying. Include any promotional materials to help a reporter be a better reporter. Provide hard copies but hang them on your web page, too, for historical reference and a place to point reporters to.
- **Have an agenda and stick to it.** This will keep you on track and help you achieve your objectives in the allotted time. Any reporter who is worth their salt will always have *one more question*, so be prepared to cut things off when you've reached your advertised time limit. I usually begin the wrap-up

with, "We have time for one more question," but can quickly end a press event if things have run long or your spokesperson is not faring so well with, "We've run out of time. Thank you for coming."

» Your first press conference may not be your only press conference. After this initial press event, you may uncover additional information worth sharing and need to schedule a follow-on press event.

» You may also discover your initial spokesperson is not your best spokesperson. After this first press conference, your speaker may need additional media training. Or you may determine there is a leadership member who would better represent your brand to the public. This becomes another opportunity to refine your diplomacy skills when making this recommendation to your leadership team.

• **Prepare your principal for the event.** Schedule a session or two with the spokesperson ahead of the press event so you know what's on their mind and can help them focus on the key points to convey to the press. You'll also review anticipated hard questions and propose ways to mitigate the negative ones.

• **Record the events.** Today, with social media, literally everything is recorded and often live-streamed. It's always good to have a designated team member to document it so you own the footage. You can use the same footage to promote the event via social media in real time and on your web page. You can also use it to fact-check coverage to ensure your principal is quoted properly and in context.

# WHAT YOU NEED TO KNOW

- Social media must be actively managed as part of your steady-state daily operations. Social media allows for direct engagement with your key audiences and may even make you aware of a developing crisis situation needing your attention. You can glean valuable information directly from your customers through social media platforms.
- Once a crisis presents itself, begin with a holding statement until you have more facts, and then send out a press release with the five Ws and H once you know more.
- If the situation escalates or deteriorates and warrants it, plan your press conference to demonstrate your awareness and active engagement to managing the crisis.
- Use your leadership team and subject-matter experts to transparently convey what your company is actively doing to manage the crisis. Tell your customers what you're doing to remedy the situation and keep it from happening again.

- You always have the option of doing or saying nothing. Weigh the risk with the chance others may fill the space in your absence.
- No matter how much you anticipate and actively manage a crisis, you'll have to remain flexible as you think through the next steps and what you need to say.

## WHERE THINGS WENT WRONG

**Bottom Line Up Front: Verify facts and spell names correctly.**

Follow these two cardinal rules in writing news releases: (1) get your facts straight, and (2) spell names correctly.

When you're performing at a high pace and intensity, like in combat, the opportunity for mistakes increases exponentially.

I had compiled a news release in Afghanistan and touched base with our German operations chief, a two-star general, prior to release. He had a few questions about the type of vehicle involved. I answered his question without thinking. I didn't double-check the information with our command center. It came back to bite me because I got it wrong and had to issue a correction almost immediately.

I felt as much embarrassment with the two-star as I did with my media operations team. My name was on the release and therefore my name was also on the one with **CORRECTED COPY** in bold at the top we had to issue hours later. While everyone makes mistakes, inaccuracies erode trust and undermine transparency. Without trust, it's next to impossible to lead effectively, especially during crises.

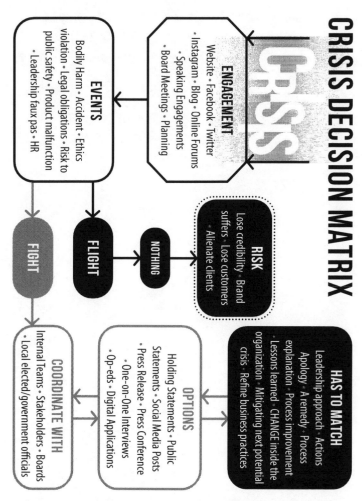

# CRISIS DECISION MATRIX

**CRISIS**

**ENGAGEMENT**
Website • Facebook • Twitter
• Instagram • Blog • Online Forums
• Speaking Engagements
• Board Meetings • Planning

**EVENTS**
Bodily Harm • Accident • Ethics
violation • Legal obligations • Risk to
public safety • Product malfunction
• Leadership faux pas • HR

**FIGHT**

**FLIGHT**

**NOTHING**

**RISK**
Lose credibility • Brand
suffers • Lose customers
• Alienate clients

**HAS TO MATCH**
Leadership approach • Actions
Apology • A remedy • Process
explanation • Process improvement
• Lessons learned • CHANGE inside the
organization • Mitigating next potential
crisis • Refine business practices

**OPTIONS**
Holding Statements • Public
Statements • Social Media Posts
• Press Release • Press Conference
• One-on-One Interviews
• Op-eds • Digital Applications

**COORDINATE WITH**
Internal Teams • Stakeholders • Boards
• Local elected/government officials

*It's tough to determine when you are in crisis. This decision matrix helps you quickly assess your situation so you can take the right course of action. Share it with the rest of your leadership team so, together, you can develop the best strategy to manage your crisis.*

*Go to* www.TheViragoCircle.com *for a downloadable copy.*

# 7

# IT'S NOT *WHAT* YOU KNOW, IT'S *WHO* YOU KNOW

**M**y time in Afghanistan bridged 2006 and 2007 and is the setting for much of what I cover in this chapter. NATO's primary focus in Afghanistan was to progress toward a secure country functioning as its own democratic republic free from terrorism or Al Qaeda. Thirty-two contributing nations developed a joint international effort to root out the Taliban and provided troops and equipment for over twenty years.

NATO coordinated with neighboring countries such as Pakistan, Turkmenistan, and Qatar to develop a war plan to optimize assets, train the Afghan forces, and leave when they were ready to handle it on their own.

To give you some background, NATO's International Security Assistance Force (ISAF) officially ended in 2014, transitioning to Operation Resolute Support on January 1, 2015. The new international umbrella was tasked with providing training, advice, and assistance for Afghan security forces and other established institutions ahead of the international departure. That drawdown began in April 2021 and was complete in September 2021.

# BUILDING COALITIONS

During the time I served with NATO in Afghanistan, relations with Pakistan were especially important as the line between Afghanistan and Pakistan was loosely drawn over steep mountain passes and low valleys. To aid in the important coordination and develop those relationships, NATO's ISAF hosted a Pakistani delegation in Kabul. The purpose was so each country could meet personally with our counterparts and improve communication. Open lines of communication were developed over an afternoon tea in a building just outside our headquarters. Then we each went back to our respective countries with a greater appreciation for the other's perspective.

Fast-forward about two weeks and I needed to coordinate a release with the same Pakistani counterpart. ISAF suspected a significant group of Al Qaeda operatives were moving along the very thin dotted line separating Afghanistan and Pakistan and were planning a mission to intervene. Out of respect for sovereign Pakistan, ISAF wanted to ensure Pakistan understood our intent well ahead of the operation taking place, but not so far in advance the mission might be compromised. Corruption was common in this part of the world, and there were operatives who played both sides against the middle. While they may be employed by their country's government, certain operatives also likely had at least one relative affiliated with the terrorists.

We had no secure communication line established between the two public affairs offices, so the coordination with Pakistan had to be done over unclassified lines. Hours before the operation took place, I sent my Pakistani counterpart a news release developed in anticipation of a successful mission. He offered no changes. Doing so late in the afternoon *before* the operation was to occur over an unclassified line was unnerving for me, to say the least. I had just established a professional relationship with my Pakistani counterpart. With this coordination, I extended an extreme degree of trust he would not share the release with anyone who might inform the insurgents. I had to trust he was being truthful and transparent, and he had to extend me the same courtesy.

You may already know from your own experience, having open lines of communication with your counterpart in business or local government is a beneficial way to strengthen your position as a professional communicator. Likewise, a professionally close relationship with members of leadership is critical. If you don't already, take the time right now to load your cell phone with contact information of key people you may need to coordinate with, inside and outside your organization, if a crisis were to present itself. Create your list of key people you know you need to reach out to and put it on the top of your punch list or to-do list.

Rehearsing for one-on-one interviews ahead of press engagements tremendously improves your ability to deliver your key points effectively. It's also during these one-on-one interviews you build a professional rapport with the reporter. As a communication or public relations professional, you straddle the space between your organization and the public you serve or provide a product for.

You have to think like your boss and you also have to think like the press does. Invest time with each of them separately at first and then bring the two of them together for a one-on-one interview before a crisis comes knocking on your door. This became clear to me when I was stationed at the Pentagon.

The Pentagon is situated in Arlington, Virginia, to allow military leaders and senior civilians providing oversight to our operations ready access to Congress. Military leaders routinely have one-on-one meetings with congressional officials to discuss programs and policies and keep them informed. Providing congressional testimony is the most public interaction military leaders have with those elected officials and requires significant preparation. Their testimony is a matter of record and live-streamed.

In the weeks and days ahead of congressional testimony, the supporting staff used a process to prepare our senior executives for the most contentious testimony on the Hill—testimony the Pentagon press corps widely covered—affectionately referred to as a murder board.

# MURDER BOARD

A murder board is a brutal training experience both for those planning the training and for the one in the hot seat. The staff prepares information the principal should know on multiple topics with a series of the hardest questions they think legislators will ask. The staff turns the tables and grills the principal, having them rehearse answering these tough questions as if they were actually delivering sworn testimony. It's rapid fire, includes real-time feedback to help those testifying refine their answers, usually lasts hours, and can be mentally exhausting for everyone involved.

For the public affairs officers or communication professionals, our contribution to the process included preparing the principal for those contentious issues or programs recently covered in the press. It took me days to compile likely interest areas leading up to the testimony. I based my prep material on stories I knew the press were interested in so I could offer the most comprehensive analysis.

I entered the conference room where our senior executive was being run through the traps. I found a room with about thirty people sitting around a long conference table, each a subject-matter expert on myriad topics. The person who was up to brief the principal sat down next to them and reviewed the seeming volumes of information about various military policies and programs. Compared to many who were to brief the principal, the media portion was short. It included contentious issues recently covered by the press, programs or issues the media were expected to ask about, and key points to make.

When it was my turn to brief, I sat down next to the principal, reviewed the reporters' biographies and recent articles they'd written for what seemed like an eternity but was really about twenty minutes while everyone in the room listened. I answered a few clarifying questions and then wrapped up.

On the day of the congressional testimony, I scoured the morning news to determine if there was anything of note to brief my executive on and used the opportunity while traveling with him to the Hill to do so. Just as we were about to enter the hearing room, as predicted, we ran into two press members who asked a few questions, conducting what is commonly known as a fly-by interview. I was pleased to hear the reporter ask questions about some of the same topics covered during the murder board. My principal delivered an answer he'd already rehearsed.

After the testimony, we gathered and analyzed the coverage. The press were factual and fair with their coverage. My principal had been quoted accurately and in the context in which he was speaking. You can't ask for much more.

The murder board is a comprehensive way to prepare your CEO or president for the toughest of press interviews they will ever undertake. While it takes a great deal of preparation to mimic what they may experience during a crisis, it is an effective way to prepare to manage it.

# WHERE THINGS WENT WRONG

**Bottom Line Up Front: "Expert in your field" does not equate to an "eloquent public speaker."**

Your CEO or president for any particular press engagement has a deeper understanding of the issues than you, the communication expert, ever will. They possess a great deal of technical knowledge they brought to their leadership position and so do you.

While they understand the mission fully and have a clear vision, they may not be naturally eloquent speakers. Convince your leaders to prepare for crisis communication a little differently and undergo some degree of media training before stepping in front of a hot mic. You will both be glad you did.

Take on the persona of the reporter and ask the tough, probing questions before the camera is on. Really try to trip them up in the safe space training affords so when they do it for real, they've got their bearings.

# WHAT YOU NEED TO KNOW

- Find out who you are most likely to collaborate with during a crisis and introduce yourself over a cup of coffee or afternoon tea. Developing relationships ahead of a crisis will prove invaluable when one hits.
- Load your cell phone with key contacts you'll need when a crisis occurs. Include your leadership team, board members, and your counterpart in government agencies or collaborating businesses you may need to call upon in a crisis. Include reporters you know you'll want to reach out to personally when a crisis occurs.
- Murder board your clients before they are forced to step behind the podium during a crisis. Rehearse the answers to the toughest of questions, so those answers will come much easier when the stress is high.
- Conduct an after-action review to assess how the coverage turned out after your engagement to refine your delivery for the next time a crisis occurs.

In the military, we have a crash kit packed and ready to go so when there is a crisis situation; we don't have to stop and think about critical things we might need to grab on our way to the scene. The crash kit includes items like a spare phone charger and reflective vest in a backpack for an inconvenient or remote location. Here is a list of items for a starter crash kit you might store in your office, car, or home. You can always add needed items depending on the type of business you work in.

## CRASH KIT ESSENTIALS

When a crisis hits, you'll be glad you have the following in a backpack, duffel bag, or tote bag ready to go.

- **Fill-in-the-blank news releases.** These are handy and are the result of the preplanning you will do before a potential crisis occurs. When you're in the middle of a crisis, it's always easier to start with something as opposed to a blank computer screen. For the military, these include templates on airplane crashes, force development changes, chemical spills, vehicle accidents, or bird strikes. Store them on Google Drive or Slack for remote and instantaneous access.

- **No Wi-Fi.** Plan for not having Wi-Fi since your crisis may occur in a remote location where the satellites don't necessarily align. While this seems old school, you may consider printing out a hard copy of select documents to have with you when you head out to the woods or the desert.

- **Flashlight** might seem old-fashioned but if your phone is in need of a charge, it might be good to have a separate flashlight. Don't forget the right **batteries** in it so it's ready to go.

- **Phone charger** and separate **battery pack**. You may have to respond for an extended period of time. Pack a **universal charger** and a **power strip**.

- **Crime tape.** While a crime may not have necessarily occurred, you may need something to cordon off the area until your recovery operations show up to analyze the physical remnants of what took place. It's just like the type they use on *NCIS* and can be bought at a hardware store or online.
- **Reflective vest.** Wearing one may keep you from being your own casualty with a press vehicle in a hurry to show up on the scene.
- **Pad of paper.** I find it's best for me to write something out freehand first to organize my thoughts. I then use a voice command to put my words into digits.
- **Pens.** Also may be considered old-fashioned but very necessary.
- **Travel toothbrush and toothpaste.** So you don't offend those you work long hours with and are ready for the spotlight when the press conference occurs. Especially if you've been drinking a lot of coffee.
- **Toilet paper.** You might laugh, especially you guys, but if you're on an accident scene out in the middle of a field, the urge may strike you. Think of an on-scene crisis as a camping trip—the better you prepare, the more pleasant the experience.
- **All-weather jacket.** Weather rarely cooperates when you are in a remote area of the woods. Have one with some warmth to it or a multi-system jacket for varying climate changes.
- **Change of clothes.** If you are on scene and have to prepare for a press event, having a change of clothes or simply a different jacket may help you better present your company.

- **Razor**. Guys may need to freshen up before stepping in front of the cameras.
- **Snacks.** You won't know the food situation or availability.

# 8

# BUILD YOUR TEAM
# AND BUILD UP YOUR TEAM

**A**re you a thermometer or thermostat? A thermometer rises and falls depending upon the temperature in the room. A thermostat, on the other hand, determines the temperature no matter what's going on in the room.

If you are a professional communicator and a crisis hits, you have to be the thermostat. You have to remain calm. You must think logically and analyze the situation you're presented with. And you have to develop possible courses of action to help you manage the crisis. Others in leadership and those on your communication or public relations team will take their cues from you, and that will deeply impact on how well you navigate through the crisis.

Have you ever heard the term *put your head on a swivel*? While it may ignite a vision of a bobblehead on a dashboard, in the military, this phrase is for the soldiers on top of the battle tank. They ride outside of the tank's protective armor and operate the gun on top, assessing possible threats as the unit makes its way forward.

This same tactic can be applied to an effective crisis strategy for your business. You have a lot to consider instantly and must develop and execute your crisis strategy on a truncated timeline. It's crucial to assess the situation quickly, have a sense of urgency, and convey the urgency to your leadership and public relations team.

# DIVISION OF LABOR

Your boss will rely on you to have the right team structure, or prioritize your own work if you are flying solo, to handle a crisis. When I was a young lieutenant in the Air Force, my first job, as I have mentioned, was as the deputy public affairs officer at a small wing in Blytheville, Arkansas, at Eaker Air Force Base. I worked for the chief of the public affairs office, my direct supervisor, who, in turn, worked for the wing commander, the top leader on base.

It's important to plan for the division of labor for when a crisis hits. We had six people at my first duty station in Arkansas: the chief, an enlisted community relations representative, two young airmen who developed the weekly newspaper, a secretary, and me. We added another enlisted member after about a year. I was the sole media representative and handled any queries received from the press until she came on board. When a crisis hit, like in Alaska when a service member was brandishing a weapon in the hospital, everyone went into crisis mode and knew their roles and communication lines. Having background information readily available was essential.

The Air Force has official fact sheets on our aircraft and major weapons systems, as well as official biographies of our leadership. Your business may have similar promotional materials press can use as source documents. If not, I would encourage you to develop some and hang them on your website. You can populate your social media platforms with them so they are readily available when a crisis breaks.

I've experienced this time and again, and you likely have as well. When I was deployed to Afghanistan, the US embassy in Kabul received an early-morning bomb threat and the alarms blared. Since the International Security Assistance Force headquarters, where I was billeted, was just down the street from the guarded and secured embassy, I rolled out of my bunk, put on my flak vest and helmet, and grabbed my weapon. Others filed out of the female dorm I was lodged in alongside me.

Ironically, the public information office's "bunker" was our office, on the second floor of our building. Without much thought to what was taking place or my own personal safety, I sat down at my computer and began reading the status reports coming out of the command center.

Because we were already in an active combat zone, this particular crisis started my day earlier than normal. Muscle memory kicked in and I and the rest of the team began gathering information, preparing a holding statement, and drafting a subsequent news release. The junior British officer developed the holding statement and our Belgian representative verified information from the command center for a lengthier release. I met several reporters just outside the gate later in the day to provide a stand-up interview about the threat, how ISAF had responded, and the impact on Kabul's security.

It's challenging to communicate for your organization but especially during combat operations since there is so much information to process and people's lives are literally at risk. You have new people rotating onto your team every six to twelve months, so you have to bring them up to speed almost immediately upon arrival. Since troops are assigned to the unit from their respective countries, I didn't have the privilege of choosing who I would work with at any given location and certainly not who would be on my team at a deployed location. As a leader, I had to assess the skills of the individual troops coming into the media operations cell and determine how they could best contribute to the mission.

# BUILD YOUR TEAM

You have likely been in a similar situation where you have to collaborate with someone you don't know well or have a new hire demanding more time and attention than you'd anticipated. Here's my approach to building the team I have, or the one I am assigned, to achieve the mission. These are tactics you can employ on your team right now before a crisis occurs and may still be implemented during a crisis, simply on a shortened timeline.

- **Communicate directly, one-on-one and as a team, and very clearly.** It takes time but it is an investment you can ill afford to neglect.

It's critical for each team member to understand what their priorities are. I recognized there was one team member in Afghanistan who needed a lot more time and attention than another. Providing more one-on-one follow-up was necessary, and the others didn't need anything but a brief conversation once a day to keep me informed of what was already accomplished toward the mission.

- **Discover what individuals are really great at and assign them those kinds of tasks.** I had a highly skilled individual in developing graphics and one who was better at writing more thoughtful pieces. I assigned them those tasks during high-stress situations because it was the most efficient and effective way to perform as a team.

- **Provide left and right parameters for your team to achieve the mission.** Provide direction and guidance, then step back and allow your team to shine. Check in regularly to see if they need anything, and keep an open door policy for them to do the same if and when they are unsure about something. When I was in Korea, United States Forces Korea launched our Facebook page. The comments received became a part of our daily stand-up if anything was percolating on the page. I was able to provide guidance if there were comments the officer-in-charge wasn't quite sure how to respond to.

- **Praise your team publicly.** Whether your leadership team has daily, weekly, or monthly touchpoints, take the opportunity to highlight a win your team experienced or a contribution they made to achieve the mission. At the end of any deployment, a commander has the opportunity to award a medal to those who have contributed significantly to achieving the warfighting mission.

  When I was in Afghanistan, I was part of the tenth wave of troops deployed there. Before troops departed and returned to their respective countries, the commander would award ISAF medals in a ceremony. Your business may award cash for increased sales or have a party to celebrate a merger with another company. For example, the owner of Spanx gave each employee a first-class destination vacation for every employee since the business was performing so well.

- **Correct them privately.** Everyone makes mistakes, but no one wants to be embarrassed in front of their peers. Pull them to the side as soon as you can with as much compassion as you can muster, given the crisis you are handling. I had a young officer whose actions were obviously negatively impacting the mission. Essentially, she was flirting with just about every guy she encountered. She was distracted from her job writing press releases and flushing out information. It also became distracting to the rest of the team who took notice. I pulled her to the side after dinner the day it became clear it was undermining our team, and I counseled her about it. I allowed her the opportunity to defend her behavior but told her the impression she was leaving on the rest of the team: she was spending more time flirting than doing her job. She didn't realize the implications her actions had on the functioning of the team.

- **Train for what they lack.** When you have those difficult one-on-one conversations, or even as part of a scheduled annual review, you may uncover skills your team may not have. This may prompt you to pursue an avenue to overcome a shortcoming. While not so easy to remedy in a wartime situation, in your steady-state operations, you have a greater opportunity to find an online course or an in-person boot camp to bring a team member up to speed in an area they lack.

- **Develop a few fun things to do on a routine basis.** When I was in Germany, we met at 7:30 a.m. on Fridays and ran one and a half miles together. Once a month, we had a Morale Moment on a Friday afternoon. Every month a different person brought some sort of fun activity or a snack for everyone to enjoy. It was a way to cap off the week before floating into the weekend.

# CASE STUDY: PAPA JOHNS

## The Setup

Papa Johns owner and primary spokesperson John Schnatter was taped on a 2018 training call uttering the N-word. The public backlash and call for his departure from the company spiraled out of control. Had it not been for his previous comments in 2017 about the NFL "debacle" between players taking a knee during the national anthem in protest and team owners hurting pizza sales, this utterance may not have gained the traction it did.

## The Response

- In the days following the training exercise, Schnatter stepped down from his role as owner and chairman of the board.
- This was an attempt to salvage the business he built from a broom closet.
- Schnatter asserted he was set up by James Stein of Laundry Service, the public relations organization hired to help the image of Papa Johns.

Three years later, Schnatter sued James Stein and Laundry Service, the public relations organization that was on the conference call conducting the training. It was the same one who leaked only a portion of the tape initially. Schnatter had always claimed he was set up. Looking back on the climate in 2018, there were so many variables working against Schnatter, too many legal ramifications to actively engage at the onset of this crisis.

## The Result

Negative.

Papa Johns went through a rebranding in 2021 and dropped the apostrophe from their name, further disassociating the brand with Schnatter. In the months following this incident and after Schnatter stepped aside, Papa Johns conducted sensitivity training across the organization. They started with leadership and leveraged their following on social media to promote their "listening tour" across all departments.

## My Take

John Schnatter did the only thing he could have done to stop the media outlash. He essentially sacrificed himself and his image in order to protect the business.

Their transparent action with the listening tour seemed to work and kept positive improvements on social media and in the news.

NBA star Shaquille O'Neal had been a board member since 2019 and owns nine franchise locations in the Atlanta area. For a cool $8.5 million, O'Neal sold the right to use his likeness and voice in their advertising. That was a genius move. While Domino's and Pizza Hut are still the front runners in global pizza sales, Papa Johns now hovers around 22 percent of the global pizza market.

# OPERATIONS TEMPO

Military leadership, much like leadership in your own organization, has an established rhythm to share information across business lines. It may be daily, weekly, monthly, quarterly, or all of those.

In combat when I was the chief of media operations and spokesperson for ISAF, the day began with the Commanders Update Assessment (CUA). Boy do we love our acronyms. Our intelligence operatives provided an assessment of targets hit and damage inflicted. Logistics gave a picture of our health on supplies and major movements of troops or resources. Communication briefed on significant technical issues. And public affairs offered an assessment of the day's news coverage.

My public affairs members who worked the night shift prepared slides, and the colonel in charge briefed them. We established a daily rhythm and held a brief every single day, except for Friday, which was the Muslim equivalent to our Sunday and a day of pseudo-rest. Our daily touchpoint was critical to providing the commander an overall picture of the theater and kept us all informed.

# MEDIA TOUR, AFGHANISTAN

One way to enhance transparency with the public is to allow press to be embedded with a unit or escort reporters within a unit for an extended period. We'd been in

Afghanistan for half a decade when I was deployed, and the media's appetite for information was extraordinary. We had a media escort approved to a number of remote locations while operations were ongoing so reporters could talk to troops in direct contact with the enemy, living in the most remote locations, and show firsthand how the effort was progressing.

Ten different reporters traveled to the southern portion of Afghanistan. The coordination needed to make this escort opportunity a reality was tedious, labor intensive, and time consuming but certainly well worth the coverage garnered. If you watched war coverage at home, you probably saw embedded reporters in numerous units.

I'll relay an instance you can probably relate to. Even if you plan effectively, things typically don't play out in real life according to what's mapped out on paper. Flights are often delayed, people are hungry, events happen earlier than you expect them to, or more likely much later than you'd anticipated.

A media escort was scheduled to take place for over two weeks in southern Kandahar province. Our colonel had returned to the states. I was now in charge and had put a very capable Australian officer on this escort. You already know how important communication is internally to your team. It's also important externally. This concept was amplified by what transpired during these two weeks in an active combat zone.

I received daily updates by phone from the Australian field officer escorting the media. He, in turn, made phone calls to units they visited to ensure air and ground transportation, food for everyone, and lodging for the night. It was no small task as he had to coordinate with many different units.

Some reporters proved to be very high maintenance. One reporter was always late for every showtime, always had a request outside of the scheduled itinerary, and made the group late on more than one occasion. Once, the scheduled ground transportation was missed entirely. If it's only one person this impacts, it's not a huge deal, but in this case, it impacted the whole group. My officer checked in with me about the extraordinary demands being placed upon him and the other reporters.

For the sake of the safety of those who were traveling in an active war zone, after talking with the officer and the reporter, I pulled her off the trip. While it was not the most popular decision I made, it was absolutely necessary. Unable to brief NATO headquarters until the following morning, I braced myself for impact. I felt strongly I had to support the good judgment of my escort officer. I had to consider the impact to the other nine media members who were being held back and made to adjust plans for the sake of this one demanding reporter.

I took some heat from NATO headquarters. They were concerned the reporter was going to write a negative piece about being tossed off the trip. This was an instance where communication inside your organization is extremely important and where you have to remain flexible. I had to bear in mind everyone's safety and make an unpopular judgment call. Even though the reporter was upset, she remained professional and kept the story about the mission.

# MEDIA ESCORT, TEXAS

On another occasion I personally provided media escort while supporting an exercise in Texas years earlier. One way the Air Force tells our story is to have media on board our aircraft so they could experience what our aircrew experience on a mission.

I'd taken a number of reporters on board an Airborne Warning and Control System (AWACS) plane as part of an exercise. This is the plane with the large dome on top sending and receiving satellite messages. AWACS was critical to a new system in testing and we wanted to demonstrate the capability from the air.

The twelve reporters and camera crew boarded the plane and took their places in the passenger seats at the rear for take-off. Once airborne, the media were allowed to talk to the twenty crew members, ask them what their role was, and capture B-roll. As airplanes often do, we experienced turbulent weather and had to return to our seats and strap in. The situation quickly deteriorated, and the air battle manager informed me we were now unable to return to our original departure location and were going to be diverted to another base.

What was first an orientation flight to show the validity of a new system became a very dramatic story of being diverted to another base. An unplanned overnight stop occurs frequently in the military, but I had twelve reporters, all with their own unique personal needs to attend to. We landed well after the dinner hour and everyone was famished. No one had a toothbrush or any other personal toiletries. How would they file their stories?

The print journalists had their laptops and needed to plug in for internet access, so they wanted access to their rooms right away. This was before current cell phones and before Wi-Fi was readily available. Even though they didn't want to, the television reporters had to hold their stories for another day. I was concerned their inability to file their story was going to become their story and negatively impact our coverage.

There was a bus waiting for us when we landed hundreds of miles from our original location. We stopped to buy a few needed toiletries and at the dining hall to eat. Once I got the media situated, I gave my headquarters and the exercise planners an update. We discussed how our return the following day would impact ops and testing. After a shower and what seemed like nothing more than a long nap, we boarded the plane early the next morning.

Concerned about the angle of their stories, I set up additional interviews with the crew on the way back to round out the story and leave the press with an overall positive impression.

# WHAT YOU NEED TO KNOW

- Keep your head on a swivel and in the game. Continually assess the crisis situation as it develops and take the appropriate action.
- Play to your team members' strengths in a crisis. Assign them their role with parameters, give them direction as a team, and communicate one-on-one as needed to keep everyone moving through the crisis.
- Your CEO or president likely has a daily meeting with the leaders in your organization or may only need a weekly touchpoint. Whatever rhythm they have established, be prepared with succinct high-level points leadership will find valuable.
- As a communication professional, you straddle the fence between adviser and leader. You are on the leadership team providing advice and counsel. You are also the leader filtering information with guidance to your communication or public relations team in handling the crisis.
- Sometimes, you have to make an unpopular decision when managing a crisis. Be decisive and be prepared to defend your decision.
- Remain flexible when something you didn't anticipate happening occurs. Be a problem solver.

- Always pack an overnight bag before boarding any airplane, whether it's a military aircraft or commercial.
- Have a sense of urgency. When a crisis happens, you have to respond quickly and divert your efforts to actively manage the crisis.

# 9

# YOU DON'T HAVE TO BE IN A WAR ZONE TO HAVE A CRISIS

You know the feeling in the pit of your stomach when the phone rings and you hear what the person is saying, but it doesn't initially register because you don't believe what they said? You might ask them to repeat themselves. You may even repeat the words out loud yourself to convince your mind what they said occurred actually happened.

Perhaps you have had to handle a crisis about someone you knew or respected and found it especially difficult to maintain your composure and communicate effectively.

I have been in several crises where I had to check my emotions and maintain my professional composure. You probably have, too, and while difficult, it can be done.

## YAK 54

It was a beautiful Sunday morning in Alaska in June, and I was anticipating my first day of vacation after a long hard winter. I had a friend arriving later in the day to stay the week. We were planning to experience all the great adventures the Alaskan outdoors has to offer: hiking, camping, fishing, and kayaking.

I had briefed my team on the projects in various stages of development. I'd been to church and then the gym and was waiting for my friend to arrive when I got a call from our command post on Elmendorf Air Force Base. We'd had an aircraft go down, and I had to report to the command post. All my plans were postponed. I made a phone call to my number two on the team and headed to the base.

When I arrived, people were swarming everywhere. The on-scene commander confirmed our three-star general, Lt. Gen. David McCloud, and a friend had been flying his personal Yak 54, and it had crashed. Despite being prepared to respond to a downed aircraft, the emotion around losing your commander was certainly a tragedy no one anticipated.

As a communication professional, a personal crisis will be the greatest test of your professional skills.

McCloud, the Alaskan Command and 11th Air Force commander, a revered leader, along with his friend, Lewis Cathrow, perished in the crash. I began gathering information regarding the crash to craft the initial news release. I had to be mindful not only of McCloud's family, but Cathrow's family. The Air Force did not have release authority to provide any information about Cathrow.

In a situation involving an accident and especially a fatality, it's critical you distribute a news release within one hour of the incident taking place. Even if it is only one simple sentence. Timely release lends to your credibility and reinforces you are being transparent and forthcoming with as much information as soon as possible.

I was not the spokesperson for the three-star general but for the commander assigned under him, and the base where the general lived and housed his plane. Fortunately, McCloud's public affairs officer was a mentor so we already had a wonderful working relationship. Together we crafted the initial news release, which was only two sentences long, based on the verifiable information from the operations representative, who had direct contact with the on-scene commander.

After drafting the release, we printed it and read it out loud for accuracy and cadence. Even the most seasoned public relations professionals overlook details in high-stress situations, so it's always good to have someone else proof your work. Once I was confident it was accurate, I shared it with the wing commander, and I had a team member release it to the press. My media chief sent it to reporters, and my web manager posted it to our web page.

The phones started ringing almost immediately as the press wanted more information. Our team fielded the calls and logged in the time the calls came in, which media agency the reporter represented, and what their questions were. This was a process outlined in our standard operating procedure (SOP) and had been practiced many times.

For military communication professionals, peacetime and wartime bring different challenges.

The tempo may be different and the intense pressure to communicate effectively in combat tests your technical skills and your ability to remain flexible and think on your feet.

# DOWNED CHOPPER

When I was deployed to Afghanistan during combat, we lost a helicopter in May 2007 in Afghanistan. It was especially difficult because one of the members who perished was on the public affairs team in Kandahar in the south of Helmand Province. I had never met the young man from Canada, Master Corporal Darrell Jason Priede, but other communication specialists in the south had. The crash happened late in the evening with only three of us on duty.

I found many instances where the initial information provided was unclear. The media operations cell had to often begin with a very general holding statement, then develop a news release with more verifiable details. Often, if the engagement was significant, it may have then warranted a stand-up interview with reporters at the gate.

In this particular instance, the helicopter went down and the Taliban almost immediately stated they shot it down. NATO forces were far superior, and while I suspected that was not the likely scenario, I had to hold comment for a couple of hours until I could verify that assertion. It didn't stop the press from calling and asking more questions, and it didn't stop them from speculating about what had happened. Those were activities outside of my control. What I could and did control was the release of factual information.

As I noted earlier, the standard for releasing information after an incident or an accident is one hour. Our command post notified the media ops cell a helicopter went down and had no further information. While the Belgian officer I was working with and I drafted the initial release, we blew the one-hour standard for distributing it, but not by much. After drafting the news release, and verifying the information with the command post, I had to check in with the night commander who was managing the aftermath of the accident.

It was the simplest of releases. A helicopter is down in the south of Afghanistan and there will be an investigation. We distributed the release and determined some hours later there were no survivors. The communication with the crew prior to the crash indicated there had been a mechanical failure of some degree. It was unverifiable at the time, so we did not release the information initially.

A subsequent release indicated such and additional information would be released after notification of next of kin. Making a statement naturally leads to additional questions. Since this was an international effort, questions arose regarding which country the deceased were from. What happened to the helicopter? Did the Taliban actually shoot it down?

Anyone familiar with the international effort knew the British, Canadian, and Americans were the forces operating in the southern part of Afghanistan. The media drew their own conclusions about the nationality of the lost crew and speculated about it in their initial reporting.

Each country maintained their individual release authority for an incident involving the death of their troops. Even though I was the spokesperson for NATO, I could not verify what I knew to be true and what the press continued to speculate about. It took days to reach all of the next of kin for those who perished in the crash in their respective countries. In the meantime, ISAF continued to provide information about the incident, and while this tragedy occurred, ISAF was still providing for the security of Afghanistan.

Since a member of our public information team died in the crash, as a leader, I had to remain mindful of the negative personal effect on the team in the south while simultaneously managing up to our high headquarters and their demand for information. It's a delicate balance as you straddle managing up to one entity while remaining compassionate to those closest to the tragedy. Our team had numerous phone calls with NATO headquarters over the next few days as more information became known and as countries verified their lost members.

I spoke with the public affairs officer in the south numerous times in the days following the crash who was understandably in shock about the tragedy. NATO headquarters was demanding information from me, and I tried to verify what they needed. I was attempting to compassionately extract information from the public affairs officer. In one conversation, he said, "Our feelings are very raw," as they grappled with what had just transpired.

It was one of the more difficult situations I have been in. I had a tingling feeling in the pit of my stomach and felt the urge to cry, but I didn't. I encouraged him to talk with someone close by about the loss, his feelings, those the whole team likely shared, perhaps a military chaplain.

As difficult as it was, I still needed to verify information for subsequent releases. Our team worked through the tragedy professionally despite the loss of someone on our team. Each of us had to deal with the loss in our own personal ways. And we had to come together as a team to push through and perform our mission.

# HOW TO HANDLE A PERSONAL CRISIS

It's tough when you're close to the crisis or you know the person at the center of it. While challenging, you must recognize your feelings. Then you have to check them, and put them aside, to get through the crisis. Depending on its severity, and your own personality, this will be more difficult for some than others. Everyone handles grief differently.

When communicating through crisis, you must maintain your composure. Remember the thermometer analogy I mentioned? You must be able to see beyond your personal feelings of loss, draw from what you already know about communicating through crisis, and manage through it. You determine the temperature. Here's how:

- Recognize your personal feelings of loss and allow yourself to grieve.
- Have a good cry—privately, not in front of the cameras, or with a trusted friend who can provide compassion.
- Verbalize how you knew the person and what they meant to you, or how close you were to them.
- Compartmentalize your feelings and set them aside.
- Pray about your loss. Seek counseling from your faith representative for help.
- Redirect your focus and energy into the crisis in front of you.

In the case of the helicopter, I confided in another officer deployed with me. With McCloud's death, I confided in a family member about what happened. In both situations, I talked through my own disbelief and grief, then carried on with the tasks in front of me. I cried in both instances to allow myself a moment's grief, unleashing my own emotions, if only for a brief time. Then I set my feelings aside to get words on paper and released to the press.

In both of these situations, I grappled with my own mortality. Some people even feel guilty for not being the one in the helicopter when it crashed. Seemingly only by chance was the photographer, and all others on the chopper, chosen for this particular mission. It could have been any other available crew, any of my team members in the south. The roles we play, the duties we perform, the schedules, and operation orders seemingly come together only by chance. When performing under this extreme stress, I did not have the luxury of time to allow for complete healing. I did take just a few moments to recognize my personal loss and the loss for those even closer to those who died.

When I returned from my deployment, counseling was available as it is to every returning service member. Simply being able to talk about what I had experienced and witnessed allowed me to come to terms with my own loss and my personal feelings.

# BE PHYSICALLY FIT

While communicating during crises ebbs and flows, there are things I've done to physically sustain myself and remain resilient to the physical and emotional demands that high operational tempo communicating often demands. Even though this is not a book about self-care, I want to address the physical and mental challenges of effectively communicating during crisis demands.

Staying in shape physically is a must in the military. To keep a fit fighting force, the military imposes weight and fitness standards on its troops, based upon height and age. To stay fit, relieve stress, build esprit de corps, and remain ready, units would run together weekly, monthly, or quarterly. In addition to these group fitness events, individuals also participate in other exercise, build it into the rhythm that fit their personal or family routines. Physical fitness is built into our military culture, much like your agency's dance parties or limbo contests.

In the high-profile, high-tempo jobs I've held, I've had to sustain myself and both my good mental and physical health for an extended period. Like when I had to travel across multiple time zones and fly aboard various aircraft just to arrive in theater ready to hit the ground running. Or when I participated in a foot patrol with the military police in Kabul, passing armed guards in every doorway, ready to engage the enemy should he show himself.

You may not have to battle war conditions, but being in a healthy physical and mental state may help you pull all-nighters gathering facts to prepare your principal for tomorrow's press conference or trek miles to reach a train derailment location.

While certain physical fitness standards may not be a condition of your employment, I'm confident you know what personal behaviors enhance your job performance. Determine what your best routines for sleep, nutrition, and exercise are so you can be the very best crisis communicator when a crisis presents itself.

I'm also a list-maker. I typically make a to-do list at the end of each workday, allowing myself the freedom to unburden my mind, wind down, relax, and eventually go to sleep. It's important for you to determine what habits help you perform at your peak and remain disciplined about them.

# WHAT YOU NEED TO KNOW

- After a tragic accident or incident involving life or limb, do all you can to make your initial media release within one hour.
- Always print out your news release and read it out loud for clarity and to catch any errors. Have a second set of eyes to help you proof and ensure there are no errors.
- Establish how you will verify information prior to release with an SOP, standard operating procedure. In combat, we relied heavily on secure communication with the ground commander through the command post. Our public affairs representative would send information to the media operations cell that ultimately wrote the news releases.
- Provide information in a graduated manner. Start with a simple, individual holding statement, then put out a follow-up news release with more facts in it, and consider live interviews to provide additional information or context to frame the story.
- Identify the partners outside of the organization you need to involve before a crisis occurs. Establish a relationship with them today so

when a crisis develops, they are a source
of support through it and can amplify your
message.
· Understand what your body and mind need to
perform at your best during a crisis. Establish
a routine with regular exercise, and remember, managing through a crisis is a marathon,
not a sprint.

# CASE STUDY: DEEPWATER HORIZON

### The Setup

On April 20, 2010, the oil drilling rig Deepwater
Horizon, operating in the Macondo Prospect in the
Gulf of Mexico, exploded and sank resulting in the
death of eleven workers. The Deepwater Horizon,
owned by Transocean but leased by British Petro-
leum (BP), was the largest oil spill in the history of
marine oil drilling operations. Four million barrels of
oil flowed from the damaged Macondo well over an
eighty-seven-day period, before it was finally capped
on July 15, 2010.

The explosion was caused by a blowout of the
wellhead more than a mile below the surface. A culture of high-risk behavior combined with the lack of
a direct chain of command on Deepwater led to the
series of events that caused the accident.

## The Result
Tragic. Eleven lives lost. Devastating environmental consequences.

## The Response
It took BP two days to issue a statement from Group Chief Executive Tony Hayward to "do everything in our power to contain this oil spill and resolve the situation as rapidly, safely and effectively as possible." They deployed a flotilla of vessels and other equipment to mitigate the damage. Despite their concerted efforts and similar public statements, it took BP three months to actually stop the oil from flowing. While BP and others were later named in a lawsuit, the company gladly paid a fine.

## My Take
BP should have exhibited a greater sense of urgency, issued an apology and condolences immediately. Once they knew and understood the cause of the explosion, BP should have held a press conference to explain the failure and steps they were taking to refine internal processes to keep this from occurring again. Three months is a long time to contain a spill, and the company should have done more to contain it sooner. Clearly, BP needs to conduct a risk assessment and change its business practices. I would recommend reviewing all internal checklists to identify areas where similar risks exist.

BP also needs to assess its chain of command and instill better processes to respond sooner should a similar tragedy occur. BP executives involved in the decision-making process at this time should be held accountable for their seemingly cavalier actions leading to the death of these eleven men.

On December 15, 2010, the United States filed a complaint in District Court against BP Exploration & Production and several other defendants alleged to be responsible for the spill. Appropriately so. The vast majority of the $69 billion tab was paid by BP with Transocean and drilling partners Anadarko and MOEX contributing.

# 10

# UNDER ATTACK: CONTROLLING THE MESSAGE WHEN THE WORLD SEEMS TO BE BLOWING UP

You know, some people say we could be a target here." My colleague in the press office at the Pentagon had just foreshadowed what was to happen to us within minutes of hijacked commercial aircraft slamming into the World Trade Center towers that fateful September 11.

I headed down the length of the press room to my desk as my phone rang. I received a call from the reporter who'd scheduled the interview with my space general who asked if, considering what was taking place in New York, our interview was still on. I confidently told him I would check with the general's office and call him right back.

No sooner had I laid the phone in the cradle than the third hijacked plane slammed into the Pentagon. It was 9:37 a.m.

The world changed forever that day.

This terrorism presented a crisis of a magnitude not yet in two decades experienced in the United States. And the unthinkable had occurred. Terrorists used commercial planes as missiles and executed an attack involving hundreds of innocent civilians. The national command authority and military planners had to think through the appropriate, deliberate response given the political climate at the time.

Communicating in crisis feels different when you are the target. With an intensity you've never experienced before, stress levels skyrocket and remain high until the threat no longer remains. September 11 was the beginning of what would become an extended public crisis the United States, the Federal Aviation Administration, the Department of Defense, and the military services had never navigated through.

Outside of the initial statement President Bush made, our national response was without public comment and included numerous entities that played significant public roles. This was one of the rare times saying nothing proved to be the best course of action.

# UNDER ATTACK

There aren't a lot of interior windows in the Pentagon. Most windows are on the outer E rings where the military's senior brass are located. Architects had included a line of windows on the Air Force press desk running the length of our office on the right side, between the third and fourth corridors, that allowed natural light to pour in.

As the phone left my hand and landed in the cradle, I felt the impact of the attack. The building physically moved. The retro metal blinds covering those windows shook fiercely. I heard them rattling. I looked up and saw them shake. As both sensations registered in my mind, I instinctively ducked under my desk. As did others.

Seconds passed. We emerged and it was obvious we should evacuate. I grabbed my purse and my phone. Theresa, a reservist who was doing her annual tour of duty, said, "We don't want to go inside toward the courtyard, we want to go to the outer ring so we aren't trapped."

It made sense to me so I followed her down the nearest stairwell and out the door of the River Entrance. Thousands more military and civilian personnel flooded out of the building alongside us.

No sooner had I cleared the doorway than my eyes floated upward to see thick black smoke billowing out over the top of the building. I heard the whipping blades of a helicopter. Was this a second wave of the attack? Who owned the helo? Was it the bad guys? I instinctively ducked again, then looking up and not falling under fire, I realized the helicopter was one of ours.

Outside of those helicopter blades, though, the scene was eerily quiet. Traffic usually buzzing by well over the speed limit on the nearby highway had ground to a halt. As I moved away from the building, I began searching for familiar faces and soon found my colleague Mike. It was only by chance I connected with others on the press desk as we had no predetermined rally point in case of an evacuation.

Even if you had cell phones, communication through them was impossible. The attempted simultaneous calls jammed the available satellite feeds. Considering the crisis in front of us and anticipating a long day, Mike nominated Theresa and me to go home and be prepared to come back to work the night shift.

# OTHER GOVERNMENT AGENCIES

Arlington police and emergency medical units responded immediately. As I rushed out of the River Entrance, the medical staff in the Pentagon's clinic headed in the opposite direction and began to treat those pulled from the building. The press covered the attack from as close as local authorities allowed, but local authorities immediately cordoned off the streets surrounding the Pentagon.

As they grappled with the possibility of additional attacks with the thousands of airborne planes, the Federal Aviation Administration took immediate action. In an unprecedented move, the FAA issued a nationwide ground stop at 9:45 a.m., preventing all civilian aircraft from taking off. Any airborne planes were forced to land at the nearest available airstrip, stranding thousands in places they'd never intended to go, creating another crisis that extended weeks after the initial attacks.

# CONTROL THE MESSAGE

The president made his initial comments and the State Department took the lead on any release of information for a little more than a week. No other government entity released any official information.

DOD had received guidance from the White House that was controlling the narrative while assessing the situation and determining the way forward. The media speculated on what we would do after such an attack. How would the United States respond? Instead of an active posture, the individual services took a passive approach and said nothing until the White House, and then the Department of Defense, deemed it appropriate before referring all media queries to them. This felt different though. Where before I was confident they would handle the press, in this instance, I knew we said nothing because we didn't know what we were going to do.

I had been accustomed to my higher headquarters taking the lead on public statements. This was one case where our national leadership saw no benefit in making extensive public statements. There were no media interviews set up in the immediate aftermath of the attacks. There were simply too many unknowns. This passive approach allowed our national command authority to gather information, assess the situation, and consider our national response. They took this deliberate, measured approach to control the narrative and it was, by and large, successful.

Controlling the message during a crisis may sometimes be the best course of action. When completely caught off guard, saying nothing provides time and space to develop your best course of action and lay a very deliberate communication strategy on top of it. How much time and space you can take depends on many factors—some you can control and others you cannot.

# WHAT YOU NEED TO KNOW

- When you are the target, your initial, instinctual response is one of self-preservation, which is entirely natural and to be expected. After the initial reaction of horror and disbelief, you must distance yourself emotionally and execute your communication strategy.
- Communicating internally with your team is critical. A weekly meeting is common in business but when you are working in a high ops tempo, a daily spin-up, even a brief one, keeps leaders informed and your team on track.
- If you don't have a rallying point and a communication plan for when you or your business is a target, think through one now.
- Despite the ready availability of cell phones, landlines or hard lines still prove valuable and needed. Immediately following the attack, satellite feeds ceased to connect because of the high demand. Since we still had a hard line in our home in Arlington, I was able to communicate with family and friends in the information vacuum.
- Recognize where you fit in the bigger picture. A national attack required coordinating extensively with other government agencies over an extended period of time: the White House, Department of Defense, the services of the Army, Navy, Army National Guard, Air

National Guard, Federal Aviation Administration, Federal Bureau of Investigation, DC Metro Police, Arlington Police Department, the Pentagon Police, and the Metropolitan Washington Airports Authority. Know who your higher headquarters is so you don't overstep your boundaries.

- Taking a passive approach—essentially refusing to comment—is one strategy providing a degree of message control until you develop a more comprehensive crisis response. This is always an option, but when you do this, understand others may fill the void.
- Remain flexible as you assess the crisis and adjust your posture accordingly.

## WHERE THINGS WENT WRONG

**Bottom Line Up Front: Culture matters.**

You must truly understand your mission, culture, and team members so you, as a public relations professional, can represent it with the greatest integrity. I made a rookie mistake when I was deployed to England during Desert Storm. After the fighting ceased, *People* magazine was interested in doing a story about our operations, specifically our B-52 pilots. It became apparent they had a misconception the B-52 crew was just like Tom Cruise in the original *Top Gun*. They are not.

The reporter asked me if they could take photos of two pilots walking toward the B-52, walking away from the B-52, and standing next to the B-52. And when I approached the pilots about this, they considered it but told me on a B-52, it's not a one- or two-man crew where you have one individual pilot in charge. For the B-52 to fly successfully and perform its mission, it takes all six crew members.

When I talked to the pilot about the media request, I was schooled up on military culture, crew integrity, and how it takes the whole team to fly the plane. This was something I hadn't considered before then. If this crew hadn't explained how we could accommodate the media with a photo op in this way, I would not have known.

There are many nuances in understanding military culture and it takes time to do so. Healthcare is a bit different from nonprofits, as are corporations and start-ups. Think through how accommodating any specific media request will be received in house and the impression it will give to your viewing or reading audience.

Talk to your boss or CEO about this to demonstrate your in-house cultural awareness. Discuss accommodating media requests—or not. Involve other members of your leadership team as you develop strategies to promote your mission or business. Doing so will help you avoid a gaffe like I experienced. It will earn you political capital and trust if you are thoughtful about this.

# 11

# PICK UP THE PIECES AND SALVAGE YOUR BRAND

Tylenol, owned by Johnson & Johnson (J&J), is still one of the most recognizable over-the-counter pain relievers today and one of the best-case studies for crisis communication still used in marketing schools.

In 1982 seven people in Chicago died, all after taking Extra-Strength Tylenol later determined to have been tampered with and laced with potassium cyanide. When investigators tied these unusual deaths to Tylenol caplet consumption, J&J took immediate action to recall all 31 million bottles on store shelves at a cost of more than $100 million.

For as many companies that fail miserably managing through crisis, many more like J&J successfully move through a crisis with their brand intact.

J&J took an active role with the media and a multipronged communication approach by issuing mass warnings. Police broadcast these urgent warnings throughout Chicago neighborhoods to keep anyone else from taking possibly contaminated medicine. J&J offered replacement capsules to those who turned in pills already purchased and a reward for anyone with information leading to the apprehension of those involved in these random murders.

J&J introduced new packaging to protect against any tampering and worked with the FDA to develop safety standards the United States still adheres to today. They took a critical look at the processes and made significant and costly changes to them. The company rebounded and returned as the bestselling nonprescription pain reliever on the market, enjoying a 35 percent market share. I believe Tylenol remains a reputable brand today because they took immediate action to protect consumers and successfully conveyed those actions to the press.

There was no way Tylenol could have forecast this crisis.

You may also find yourself charting new territory when communicating for a company with a crisis they'd never anticipated. Have you ever felt as if you're starting off yet already behind the eight ball? What do you do when you step into a crisis already in full swing or, like Tylenol, try to recover after a tragedy when your brand's reputation has already suffered damage? How will you ever get a handle on what has already transpired so you can provide the valuable crisis communication strategy your boss needs?

# THE AFTERMATH OF A CRISIS

When I returned to Ramstein Air Base, Germany, after being in Afghanistan for seven months, I stepped into the aftermath of a crisis I had no idea had taken shape.

Ramstein and the neighboring Landstuhl Regional Medical Center are often the first stop for casualties returning from the fight. This area in Germany is also the most densely populated area with a military presence overseas. Military planners considered both these facts and decided to attach a mall to a hotel near the airfield. This would not only better serve transitioning service members, but the large military population on Ramstein and other bases throughout Germany. It seemed to make sense.

However, the United States military was paying millions of euros for this combined military hotel and mall, and the Kaiserslautern Military Community Center (KMCC), a construction project funded through multiple US government sources, was way over budget and way behind schedule.

CBS's long-standing Sunday evening show *60 Minutes* and their exposé "Fleecing of America" had aired right before I returned from my deployment. Congressional testimony on the beleaguered project had already taken place on the Hill. The KMCC was delayed, over budget, at least a national embarrassment, and, according to *60 Minutes*, might involve some degree of criminal activity.

A major complicating factor was the project included multiple funding streams from across the Department of Defense. Complicating the funding streams was the fact that Ramstein was located in another country. Paperwork was done in another language requiring translation, construction processes were different, and as a result, project timelines were longer. Oversight required coordination with each agency invested in the project, and the fluctuating exchange rate complicated funding even more.

While invoices were translated into English, the work orders themselves were between two German entities and, therefore, not translated into English. Simply put, the description on the work orders did not match the invoicing. Instead of holding the invoice until such time as the work was actually accomplished, the US military was encouraged to make payment with the understanding the work orders would catch up to the invoices. Payments were made and, in turn, the US military asked for reimbursement from those other government agencies involved in the project.

This flawed process had been going on for at least two years and was one of the root causes of the stalled construction, along with the lack of American oversight.

US military leadership and the German Ministry of Defense and Ministry of Finance began to develop a strategy to move this behemoth of a project open for business. Negotiations began shortly after I returned from Afghanistan, and I became the single communication point of contact for what United States Forces in Europe would say publicly in the wake of the *60 Minutes* piece.

# TAKE STOCK

When you find yourself tossed into a crisis, the first thing you have to do is take stock of where you are and develop a deliberate strategy going forward. Ask a lot of questions and understand what your boss or

CEO expects on the back end of the crisis. In this case, the desired outcomes were a finished mall and hotel under budget.

Some leaders feel as if they have to do something, almost anything, to manage the genie already released from the bottle. For communicators, sometimes the less you say, the better, which proved the best posture in the aftermath of this crisis. I opted for a passive response-to-query approach. There would be no active media engagement, and any release of information would be coordinated between USAFE and the German Ministry of Finance.

A task force of representatives from the various agencies involved was dispatched from the United States to Ramstein: the Department of Defense, the Air Force, Morale Welfare & Recreation and Non-Appropriated Fund offices. This initial task force stayed in Germany for a little more than two weeks. Our vice commander met with the Ministry of Defense and Ministry of Finance, the head of civil engineers, the current KMCC project officer, a number of attorneys, and more civil engineers and public affairs liaisons. These representatives toured the project site, had multiple meetings to understand what had transpired and to document what they learned, and ultimately returned to the United States.

During the initial investigation, it became clear the military would receive an invoice from the German construction company on contract to do the build, but the actual work had not yet been performed. The Air Force had to own up to their flawed process, admit our error in how work orders were processed, and actually tie them to invoices. The United States government owned that error, as *60 Minutes* had clearly reported.

I, along with a number of civil engineers and attorneys, remained at Ramstein and became KMCC Task Force 2.0. Our mission was to document the root causes of the project and what remedies were needed to complete it and keep a debacle of this magnitude from ever happening again.

Instead of returning to the current operations division of our headquarters public affairs office, I was detailed to this task force full-time. The investigation into the root causes and how the military would keep future projects of this scale on track required a focused effort. I stepped out of my career field and jumped into the world of civil engineers and project management. Communication among the task force members was critical, and personalities drove the report writing and process refinement.

# MANAGING UP TO A NEW BOSS

I now had a new boss to manage. Neither of us had worked together before. Neither of us had a project of this magnitude so far behind, so over budget and such a public embarrsssment. We had to consider the public affairs implications of construction projects and the messaging needed for our task force efforts. We discussed his expectations, our processes, and our timeline for completing the KMCC task force report. I had to develop trust not only with him but with the other task force members.

We established a rhythm for investigating and documenting what would become our report of the KMCC gone awry. Because of the delicate nature of the multi-agency project and our host nation, the vice commander became intimately involved in the report writing. This ultimately slowed the process. We scheduled additional meetings to negotiate our way out of this situation with our German counterparts. It took time and patience. Stress levels and anxiety remained high as some members felt as though their careers were on the line.

After some time and further investigation, it became clear the project had been waylaid primarily because the German construction company performing the build was submitting invoices for work not actually completed. Clearly, language was a part of the challenge as the vice commander demanded all work orders would now be translated from German to English. This presented a delicate situation for the US military and our German hosts as it would take time and additional resources to interject this into the process.

Germans and Americans had a long-term relationship both were committed to, but, admittedly, the relationship was on the rocks. The stalled construction project made it seem as though neither was paying attention or actively managing it.

The core team began our investigation. We asked clarifying questions primarily of the civil engineers involved in the project, coordinating with other offices as needed, and wrote a report narrative. It was a tedious process. Military leadership refused any further release of US funds until there was a line-for-line accounting of work and the backlogged invoices were clear. This took nearly a year. The vice commander remained adamant the United States military and US taxpayers would not pay more than the original negotiated price.

# PASSIVE RESPONSE TO MEDIA INQUIRY

The communication strategy had to be palatable to both organizations. So, while negotiations on a solution were taking place, USAFE would only release information if our German counterparts agreed to the language, and vice versa. As the public affairs professional on the task force, I took a passive response-to-query stance for a year, working directly with the Minister of Finance on any releasable information. Only two German newspapers followed up with questions about the project status. I drafted the response in English and provided it to the Ministry of Finance. Once we had agreed on the language, they translated it and made the release in German.

I did receive a number of media inquiries from a weekly US newspaper intermittently. Most information requested was about where we were in the building process, when the payment would be complete, and when the mall would be open. I continued to coordinate releasable information between our American and German teams. Based on substantiated information, and working with my subject-matter experts in civil engineering, I'd craft the responses and send them to the vice commander to review before releasing them.

With only two queries from the German press, it was obvious they were not terribly interested in following the story too closely. The German government ultimately took responsibility and infused 25 million euros to essentially erase the invoice backlog and finish the project.

## WHAT YOU NEED TO KNOW

- When you step into the aftermath of a crisis, take stock of the situation and develop a deliberate strategy for recovery.
- Transparency is important. When something bad has happened, own up to it as soon as possible and demonstrate how you are correcting your mistake.
- A passive response-to-query posture may be the best approach to your post-crisis phase. Since the damage has been done, this posture may allow for message refinement and controlling the narrative.
- When you identify a problem with your process, change it, and communicate the

improved process. Show how you have implemented changes so the mistake will not occur again.

- When working with different government entities, have a clear understanding of legal obligations or other requirements and communicate differences up front.
- When working internationally, translation into English is critical.

## WHERE THINGS WENT WRONG

**Bottom Line Up Front: Close the loop.**

I learned a valuable lesson about halfway through the report writing for the KMCC.

One specific query came in the week before Thanksgiving. I tried to coordinate what I believed were the right answers first with my counterparts in civil engineering, and then with the vice commander. Despite my best efforts, he and the Minister of Finance were both unreachable, and I was unable to respond by the reporter's deadline.

The story ran the following week with a "no comment from the KMCC Task Force." This quote would not have appeared had I followed through to meet the deadline. I didn't circle back with the reporter and let him know I couldn't provide an update, nor did I negotiate to push the story another week. I could have provided a very vanilla statement to offer some sort of comment, with the promise of more details the following week.

The lesson learned is you always circle back with reporters, even if it's to tell them you have nothing to provide them and, one way or another, inform your boss of what's going on.

# CASE STUDY: VOLKSWAGEN

### The Setup
Volkswagen altered emissions tests to meet US standards in the hopes of an increase to their market share.

### The Result
Negative.

The Environmental Protection Agency determined Volkswagen intentionally programmed their turbocharged direct injection diesel engines to activate emissions controls only during lab testing, seriously tarnishing a brand they had built up to 500,000 cars annually.

This deliberate action to skirt American standards was dishonest and likely the result of executives wanting to outsell all other global automakers by sheer numbers. They violated the Clean Air Act, greatly polluting America's air, which may be linked to serious health issues in areas where they have the greatest concentration of diesel engines.

## The Response

"We've totally screwed up," said Volkswagen America boss Michael Horn, while the group's chief executive at the time, Martin Winterkorn, said his company had "broken the trust of our customers and the public." According to a BBC News report by Russell Hotten, Winterkorn resigned as a direct result of the scandal and was replaced by Matthias Mueller, the former boss of Porsche.

## My Take

Breaking the law is one thing but doing so in such a deliberate way indicates to me they have a culture and leadership problem.

Good on the leadership for admitting the screw-up. Such a deliberate criminal act indicates a greater integrity problem in the culture with certain leadership they removed.

With their brand tarnished, they have abandoned the diesel engine market and are pursuing more US sales in the growing sport utility vehicle market. Wise choice.

# 12

# CALL TO ACTION

**E**very crisis is unique. The actions you may take are often quick and fluid, and the words you choose to convey your remedy are critical.

My goal is to provide you with practical advice to guide you through your next crisis. Every crisis demands your full attention. There are things you can do today to better prepare for when the inevitable occurs, and you are involved in a serious crisis taking shape in a very public way. Do the work today to help you prepare for and better manage the crisis. You may find you even improve on your brand despite the crisis or possibly even because of it.

We all have fears, and we all have doubts. I've been precisely where you are right now, and, like you, I know the stakes are high. I'm also confident you can actively manage your next crisis, and your brand, business, or agency can become an even better one than before the crisis occurred.

It takes courage and tenacity to interject yourself into the crisis equation so you can positively affect the outcome. You now possess powerful tools, tactics, and strategies you can use today to be a more effective crisis communicator.

I wish you every success as you build your reputation as the go-to crisis communicator in your organization and industry.

# REFERENCES

Bogel-Burroughs, Nicholas. "Louisville Officer Who Shot Breonna Taylor Will Be Fired." *New York Times*, 29 December 2020. *https://www.nytimes.com/2020/12/29/us/louisville-officer-fired-jaynes-breonna-taylor.html.*

Evich, Helena Bottemiller and Meredith Lee. "FDA Refuses to Tell Congress Why Infant Formula Response Took Months." POLITICO, 19 May 2022. *https://www.politico.com/news/2022/05/19/fda-refuses-to-tell-congress-why-infant-formula-response-took-months-00033805.*

"BP Initiates Response to Gulf of Mexico Oil Spill: News and Insights: Home." BP Global, 22 April 2010. *https://www.bp.com/en/global/corporate/news-and-insights/press-releases/bp-initiates-response-to-gulf-of-mexico-oil-spill.html.*

Costello, Darcy. "Louisville Metro Police Chief Steve Conrad Fired after David McAtee Shooting, City Unrest." *Courier Journal*, 1 June 2020. *https://www.courier-journal.com/story/news/local/2020/06/01/lmpd-chief-steve-conrad-fired-after-david-mcatee-breonna-taylor-deaths/5311703002/.*

"Deepwater Horizon—BP Gulf of Mexico Oil Spill." US Environmental Protection Agency, 31 August 2022. *https://www.epa.gov/enforcement/deepwater-horizon-bp-gulf-mexico-oil-spill.*

"Dynamic Signal Report: The State of Workplace Communications Is Disconnected." *Dynamic Signal Report: The State of Workplace Communications Is Disconnected | Business Wire*, 18 April 2017. *https://www.businesswire.com/news/ home/20170418005929/en/Dynamic-Signal-Report -State-Workplace-Communications-Disconnected.*

Goleman, Daniel. *Emotional Intelligence*. Random House, 1996.

Hoffman, Carl. "Special Report: Why the BP Oil Rig Blowout Happened." *Popular Mechanics*, 2 September 2010. *https://www.popularmechanics.com/ science/energy/a6065/how-the-bp-oil-rig-blowout -happened/?utm_source=google&utm_medium =cpc&utm_campaign=arb_ga_pop_md_pmx_us _urlx_18343789675&gclid=CjwKCAiAmuKbBhA2Ei wAxQnt70zk1S67F2Kq7EqWDXPAjv_-d69fTk6m niM3VroU4WvhSi27hi_Z-BoCUGQQAvD_BwE.*

Hotten, Russell. "Volkswagen: The Scandal Explained." BBC News, 10 December 2015, *https://www.bbc. com/news/business-34324772.*

Hutchinson, Bill, and Sabina Ghebremedhin. "Former UCLA Soccer Coach to Plead Guilty in 'Varsity Blues' College Admissions Scandal." ABC News, 21 April 2020. *https://abcnews.go.com/US/ ucla-soccer-coach-plead-guilty-varsity-blues -college/story?id=70264819.*

"Kentucky Governor Has Called on the National Guard to Help Keep the Peace in Louisville." CNN, 30 May 2020. *https://www.cnn.com/us/live-news/george-floyd-protests-05-30-20/h_0df238aa3065fd3730ece5acbf2ba1f7.*

Lee, Meredith. "FDA Baby Formula Review Spares Specific Blame Amid Ongoing Shortages." POLITICO, 20 September 2022. *https://www.politico.com/news/2022/09/20/fda-baby-formula-review-ongoing-shortages-00057818.*

Leo, Leroy, and Amruta Khandekar. "Abbott Aims to Recapture Baby Formula Market Share." Reuters, 20 July 2022. *https://www.reuters.com/business/healthcare-pharmaceuticals/abbott-raises-2022-profit-forecast-2022-07-20/.*

Markel, Howard. "How the Tylenol Murders of 1982 Changed the Way We Consume Medication." *PBS News Hour*, 29 September 2014. *https://www.pbs.org/newshour/health/tylenol-murders-1982.*

Miller, Donald. *Building a Story Brand: Clarify Your Message So Customers Will Listen.* HarperCollins Leadership, 2017.

Nierman, Evan. "Council Post: Preemptively Planning for a PR Crisis: How to Protect Your Company." *Forbes*, 5 October 2020. *https://www.forbes.com/ sites/theyec/2020/10/05/preemptively-planning -for-a-pr-crisis-how-to-protect-your-company/? sh=418300a21a55.*

Richer, Alanna Durkin. "Operation Varsity Blues: Jorge Salcedo, Former UCLA Coach, Gets 8 Months in Prison for Admissions Scam." Masslive, 20 March 2021. *https://www.masslive.com/boston/2021/03/ operation-varsity-blues-jorge-salcedo-former -ucla-coach-gets-8-months-in-prison-for-admiss ions-scam.html.*

Schnatter, John. "Bombshell Recording Exonerates Papa John's Founder of Racism Claims, Alleges Set-up by Ad Firm Hired by Former Company CEO, Steve Ritchie." CISION, PR Newswire, 30 March 2021. *https://www.prnewswire.com/news-releases/ bombshell-recording-exonerates-papa-johns-fou nder-of-racism-claims-alleges-set-up-by-ad-firm -hired-by-former-company-ceo-steve-ritchie-30 1259031.html.*

Sheridan, Marcus *They Ask, You Answer, A Revolution- ary Approach to Inbound Sales, Content Marketing, and Today's Digital Consumer.* John Wiley & Sons, 2019.

"Social Media Fact Sheet." Pew Research Center: Internet, Science & Tech, 7 April 2021. *https://www. pewresearch.org/internet/fact-sheet/social-media/.*

"The Top 10 Social Media Platforms in 2023." *Shopify*, 1 November 2022. *https://www.shopify.com/blog/ most-popular-social-media-platforms.*

"USC Information on College Admissions Issue." USC Commitment to Change, 15 April 2022. *https:// change.usc.edu/usc-information-on-college-adm issions-issue/.*

Whitten, Sarah. Papa John's Blames NFL Leadership for Lackluster Pizza Sales as Shares Sink More Than 11%. CNBC, 1 November 2017. *https://www. cnbc.com/2017/11/01/papa-johns-slams-nfl-leader ship-for-lackluster-pizza-sales.html.*

# ACKNOWLEDGMENTS

**A**ny author worth their salt recognizes they are a far better writer by exposing their art to a select few trusted individuals. These people have made me a better human by participating in my life, and their perspective and expertise have improved this product in countless ways.

My sister, Kristie Crenshaw, who arguably knows me better than anyone on the planet and is the keeper of oh so many secrets. You have helped me through countless struggles and every stage of life, and I love you dearly.

Brandi Rimpsey, whose pure talent and fierce loyalty continue to amaze me. Your interest and encouragement challenged me to remain true to my art, and I treasure you.

My dear friend Vivian Hamilton for lending your expertise to this project early on. You demand excellence of everyone around you, and like so many others, I'm a stronger professional because of you.

Natalie Lohman, a friend of colossal magnitude. You create energy with your zest for living life to the fullest and your extraordinary planning skills. Few people are a friend such as you, and I am grateful for our many shared experiences.

Nancy Combs, you mentored me as a young officer and continued our friendship beyond our shared military service. Thank you for lending me your analytical skills. In doing so, you exposed the inner artist I didn't know I had in me.

Carla Givens, you bring logic and sound reasoning to everything, which has improved my life exponentially. I so appreciate you and value your friendship.

Cathy Fyock, my book coach. You gave me a safe place to create and showed me that I did have a book within me. I know I can and have changed the world, one word at a time.

Jennifer Lovett, your honesty and encouragement through the publishing process guided me through these uncharted waters. You continue to inspire me and my craft with your go-getter attitude few can replicate.

Thanks to Sandra Wendel. Your pragmatic approach to editing got me to this finished product with my sanity in check.

My mother, Margaret Hicks, and late father, Joseph Harold Hicks. You nurtured my inner artist in my formative years and encouraged me to take flight from our small town at precisely the right time.

My daughters, Annaliese and Isabel, who I know are watching my every move, and who make me a better person and Christ follower every day. I experience a joy through you and your lives that remains unmatched by any other emotion.

And my husband, Greg, who remains my number-one fan, who listens patiently to my animated tirades, and who encourages me to express my true self. I have the freedom I have in life because of your deep, unending love.

# ABOUT THE AUTHOR

ngela Billings, US Air Force veteran, strategic communicator, entrepreneur, speaker, and now author, has performed in many high-profile positions while serving in the Air Force, including communicating internationally in Germany, Korea, and Afghanistan, and as the senior Air Force representative in New York City.

Angela recognizes the power of words, how they create possibilities and achieve business goals. As an entrepreneur, strategist, and business leader, she is a master communicator who has coached military officers and executives and was an Air Force spokesperson for over twenty years.

She has prepared clients for media interviews and congressional testimony in the United States, Germany, Korea, and Afghanistan. A powerful speaker, Angela provided operational updates to military and civilian leaders from the thirty-two contributing nations of NATO's International Security Assistance Force in London in 2007. She provided leadership and communication training to Republic of Korea officers while at United States Forces Korea, Seoul, Korea.

From Germany, Angela deployed to Kabul, Afghanistan, and served as the international media chief and spokesperson for NATO's International

Security Assistance Force. She managed an international team of communicators and provided daily press updates in an active war zone.

Upon her return, Angela was instrumental in the German Ministry of Finance infusing 25 million euros into stalled construction on the Kaiserslautern Military Community Center and managed the public elements in the aftermath of that crisis first exposed on the CBS News show *60 Minutes*.

Angela is a diplomatic communicator with first-hand experience crafting language that conveys important details while still protecting classified and sensitive information. Her approach is to engage early and often in public spaces. In her view, it is far better to tell your story and manage the narrative than have someone else fill the gap.

This active yet measured approach has helped Angela weather the toughest of public relations storms: the September 11, 2001, terrorist attacks on the Pentagon, airplane crashes, base closures, force reshaping, unit deployments, troops in contact, and downed helicopters in combat against the Taliban.

After more than twenty-two years in the Air Force, Angela retired from active-duty service. Since then, Angela has worked with the University of Louisville and Frazier Rehab, Flaget Memorial Hospital Foundation, Visually Impaired Preschool Services, and the Jefferson County Republican Party and is currently the director of communication for the Kentucky Senate Majority.

She started her business, The Virago Circle, in October 2020, and speaks to leaders about effective crisis management.

Angela lives in Louisville, Kentucky, with her husband, Greg, daughters Annaliese and Isabel, and cat, Loki.

# CONNECT WITH ANGELA BILLINGS

You are invited to become a member of The Virago Circle. Go to Angela's website,

*www.TheViragoCircle.com*

and sign up for free materials she shares on crisis management.

Made in the USA
Monee, IL
29 July 2024

62881294R00120